IdentiNova

Built, Not Broken

Rebuilding Who You Are

The Companion to the IdentiNova Workbook

Alfred Brissette Jr.

Disclaimer: This book is intended for educational and informational purposes only. It reflects the author's own experiences, recollections, and opinions, and it is not a substitute for professional medical, psychological, legal, or other professional advice. The IdentiNova framework is offered as a complement to professional care, not a replacement for it. Nothing in this book should be used to diagnose or treat any medical or mental-health condition. Readers are encouraged to consult a qualified professional about their individual circumstances, and anyone in crisis or considering harming themselves should seek immediate help from a qualified provider or emergency services.

Some names and identifying details have been changed to protect the privacy of the individuals involved. The author and publisher make no guarantee as to the results any reader may achieve, and assume no responsibility for actions taken on the basis of the information in this book.

Published by IdentiNova.

ISBN: 979-8-9967840-6-6

Library of Congress Control Number: 2026918097

First Edition

First printing, 2026

If you have ever felt like you're living as someone you never quite chose to be, this book is for you. Your identity was built, mostly by circumstances you didn't pick, exactly the way everyone's is, and it makes no difference whether it was shaped by something that once devastated you or by the ordinary accidents of an everyday life. My own journey to this work was a hard one, and it's what created IdentiNova, but I share it only as proof of what's possible, never as a price you have to pay to belong here. You have your own journey, and whatever it has been, this was written for you.

A Letter to the Reader

Before you begin, I want to say a few things to you directly, the way I would if we were sitting across from each other. I don't know your story. But I know something about where a book like this tends to find a person: at a low place, or a turning point, carrying more than you let most people see, wondering somewhere underneath whether real change is still available to someone like you. I spent most of my life in that exact wondering, so I am not writing to you from above it. I am writing from the far side of it. I didn't write this book for applause, and I didn't write it to sell you a miracle. I wrote it because people kept asking me how. How I got out. How I rebuilt a life from the kind of wreckage that usually keeps a person down for good. For years I answered one person at a time. Eventually I understood that what I had been describing was a real path, with real steps, and that keeping it to myself was a kind of selfishness I could no longer justify. So I wrote it down. What you are holding is the result. I want you to know where I'm standing when I say all this. Most of what I understand about rebuilding a self, I learned the hard way, with almost nothing to build from, in the years I spent locked up for the worst thing I have ever done. I don't tell you that to make my survival into something to look up to. I tell you because it is the only thing that makes my voice worth your time here. If a person can be rebuilt from where I started, then nothing about where you are can put it out of reach. Here is the heart of it, the thing this whole book exists to show you. You are not broken. I know that word gets used, and maybe you have used it about yourself. But you were built, like all of us, out of things you never chose, and anything that was built can be built again, on purpose, by you. That is not a slogan to me. It is the truest thing I know, and I had staked my life on it long before I ever wrote a word of it down. What you do with any of this is yours, completely. I won't push you toward it. I will only tell you, with everything I have, that it is real, and then let you decide in your own time. Keep what serves you, set the rest aside, and go at whatever pace is yours. This is your work, and it was always going to be. Thank you for opening it.

Alfred Brissette Jr.

Contents

Contents

Introduction

Why This Book Exists

✦

You've probably tried to change before, really tried, and watched it not hold.

Most people who pick up a book like this have. You decided to become more disciplined, or to stop the thing you keep doing, or to finally be different in some way that mattered to you. And maybe it worked for a while. A week, a month, a good stretch. Then the old self quietly came back and took the wheel again. If that's happened to you enough times, you've likely drawn the conclusion almost everyone eventually draws: that this is just who you are. That some people get to change, and you're not one of them.

I want to tell you, as early and as plainly as I can, that I don't believe that. And I have better reasons than optimism for not believing it.

I'm not writing this from a comfortable distance. I built the framework this book is about because I needed it to survive my own life: a life that, by any reasonable accounting, should have ended me or hardened me past the point of return. I'll tell you about that life soon, not to impress you and not to ask for your sympathy, but because the whole thing rests on it. For now it's enough to say this: if change of the deepest kind were impossible, I wouldn't be here to write this, and there would be no framework to write about.

That framework is called IdentiNova. At its simplest, it's a way of understanding and rebuilding identity: eight phases that carry a person from seeing clearly what shaped them through to becoming someone they actually chose to be. That's the whole of it in a sentence. The rest of this book is what that sentence means, where it came from, and why you can trust it.

✦ What you're holding is a companion to the IdentiNova workbook, and the two do different jobs. It's worth knowing which is which before you begin.

The workbook is the doing. It walks you, step by step, through the eight phases: the actual work of understanding what shaped you and rebuilding who you are, one exercise at a time. This book is the why and the how. It's the deep dive into where IdentiNova came from, why it exists, why it works, and why it deserves your trust: the thinking and the living that sit underneath the exercises. The workbook gives you the reps. This book gives you the reasons.

You don't need to own the workbook to read this one. If you do, the two are meant to sit side by side. And if you've never seen the workbook, if you picked this up mainly to decide whether any of it is worth your time, that's fine too. I wrote this book to stand on its own, to be read by anyone trying to work out whether a framework like this could possibly be real.

Because the question of whether it's real is the one I take most seriously, let me set the terms now, before you've invested a single hour.

I came to everything in this book by living it first, and only later found that the research had been saying the same things for decades. So when I lean on science, understand what I'm doing and what I'm not. I'm not handing you studies that prove my framework works; I haven't run those studies, and I won't pretend I have. I'm showing you the places where what I lived, alone and the hard way, lines up with what trained people discovered from the outside. That convergence is my evidence, and I'll make the full case for it later in these pages. I'll also hold to honest language the entire way: this framework is grounded in and consistent with established research, not clinically proven, and I'll never blur the difference between those two things.

There's one more line I won't wait to say, because it matters more than any other in this book: what I'm offering is a complement to professional care, not a substitute for it. If you're carrying real wounds (and if you're here, you may well be), the work in these pages belongs alongside a doctor, a therapist, a genuine source of support, never instead of them. I'll explain why, in full, when we get there. But you deserve to know it from the first page.

✦ So who did I write this for? Two people, mostly.

The first is the person in the struggle: the one who has tried to change and watched it slip, who quietly suspects they might be too far gone or too far behind, who doesn't need another pep talk but an honest path drawn by someone who has actually walked it. If that's you, this book is yours first, and I wrote every page with you in mind.

The second is the skeptic. Maybe you're a clinician. Maybe you're simply someone trained to be wary of frameworks built by people without the usual letters after their name. I'm not going to court you out of that wariness, and I won't pretend to credentials I don't have. I'll tell you plainly what this is and let it stand: a bridge built to work alongside professional care, never in place of it, by someone who lived from the inside the thing the clinic studies from the outside. I make that case in full in the pages ahead.

Here's what I'll promise you, and it's deliberately modest, because the immodest promises are the ones that have already failed you.

This book won't fix you, because you aren't broken and there's nothing in you to fix. It won't change you while you read it; reading has never changed anyone. What it will do is show you, as clearly and as honestly as I can, that the self you've been living as was built, usually under conditions you never chose, and that what was built can be understood and then rebuilt on purpose. It will show you that this isn't my theory alone, but a place where one hard life and a great deal of careful research arrive at exactly the same conclusion. And it will lay out a path, in a particular order, that was walked all the way through before it was ever written down.

I'll tell my own story across these pages, because the framework came out of it and there's no honest way to separate the two. But I've worked to tell it straight: not dramatized, not cleaned up, not arranged to make me look like more than I am. There are things in my past I'll name and refuse to excuse, because the whole framework depends on the difference between understanding something and excusing it. You'll see that line held everywhere in this book. It's the spine of the entire thing.

Everything here rests on a single fact: I lived it before I built it. So that's where we'll begin: not with the framework, but with the life it was carved out of, and the long road to the moment it finally had a name.

The second [illegible]

[illegible]

[illegible] the [illegible] pages [illegible]

[illegible]

[illegible]

[illegible] down.

[illegible]

[illegible]

[illegible]

Before It Had a Name

How IdentiNova Was Lived Before It Was Built

✦

I need to be clear about one thing before I tell you any of this.

IdentiNova didn't begin as an idea. It didn't start in a classroom, a clinic, or a book I read. It began as a life, mine, lived for a long time without a map, and only much later understood well enough to draw one.

What you worked through in the workbook is that map. Eight phases, in order: Imprint, Deconstruct, Expose, Nullify, Transcend, Install, Test, Yield. On the page it looks orderly. It wasn't orderly to live. I crossed the whole territory before I had a single word for any part of it. The framework is what I found when I went back, years later, and traced a path I had already walked, not to make my life sound like a plan, but because the path turned out to be one other people could walk too.

So this chapter is the path. The rest of the book is the framework. I'm telling you where it came from not to put my life at the center. My life isn't the point. I'm telling you because a method for rebuilding identity should be honest about where it was tested. This one was tested on me first, all the way through, before I ever offered it to anyone else.

A note on how I'll tell it. I'm not going to use the hardest parts of my life for effect. There's no version of this where the pain is the selling point. I'll say what happened plainly, say what I concluded from it, and move on. And there's one fact I hold before all the others, which I'll come to, and which I won't dress up or explain away.

What shaped me

My father left when I was eight. I can't tell you the exact words he used on his way out; I've never been certain of them. What I can tell you is what I came away believing: that I was the reason he went. Whether he said something like that, or whether my mind simply reached for the nearest explanation, I don't know. A child tends to point the blame inward when something like this happens; on some level it can feel safer than the alternative. Either way, the belief took hold, and I had no way to weigh whether it was true. So I didn't weigh it. I absorbed it.

After he left, the one person who still felt safe was my brother. I followed him everywhere. He was an altar boy, so I wanted to be one too, not out of any feeling about church, but because it kept me near him. Not long after I signed up, he moved out to go live with my father. About a month after that, the abuse began. It went on for close to two years.

I'm not going to detail that here. What matters for this book is what it did to the way I understood myself. I had been a kid at the center of a big, loud family that loved to gather and celebrate. After it started, I couldn't stand to be seen. I became convinced that people could somehow tell: that if anyone really looked at me, they would know. So I shrank. Being noticed became more frightening to me than what was actually happening. I learned to take up less space, to need less, to keep quiet, to disappear inside a room I was standing in.

Three things settled into me in that stretch, and they ran my life for decades without my consent or my awareness: *I'm the reason people leave. I'm not worth staying for. Being seen is dangerous.* I didn't decide any of that. A child doesn't sit down and choose conclusions like these. He inherits them from what's happening to him and calls them the truth.

I wouldn't have a name for any of this for thirty years. It was the first thing the framework would eventually call *Imprint*: what shaped you, before you ever chose anything.

What I did with it

I ran away at eleven, because I couldn't take the abuse anymore. There wasn't much to run from at home, either; my mother worked long hours to keep us afloat, and I had been raising myself for a while.

Down by the train tracks I met a group of kids who were drinking. One of them said he knew me from the neighborhood and waved me over. Someone handed me a bottle. After a few drinks, the weight I had been carrying since I was eight lifted. I stopped scanning. I stopped feeling watched. For the first time in years I felt like I belonged somewhere, and no one asked me a single question about where I had been.

I want to be precise about this, because it's the part people get wrong. I didn't get addicted to alcohol. I got addicted to the absence of myself, and to being let in without having to explain anything. At fourteen I found drugs, and eventually a combination that worked better than anything had. From there, relief organized my whole life around itself. Small crimes. Fights. A bad divorce at twenty that sent the drinking and the drugs through the roof, and a stretch of months living on the street: a few of them in an old concrete foundation dug into a hill by the tracks, maybe six feet by five, that at least kept me dry. Then couch to couch until the people I had let down stopped opening the door, and they were right to. Much of my early twenties I simply don't remember. I'm not going to make that sound tragic and poetic. It's just gone.

The fact I hold first

There was a night, years ago, when someone lost their life because of my actions and inactions.

I'm not going to tell you the details. Not because I'm hiding from them: I gave a full account to the people who needed one, I pleaded guilty, and I served fifteen years. I keep the details out of this book on purpose, for two reasons.

The first is that a method for changing your life should never trade on the worst night of someone else's. There was a real person at the heart of it. They had a name and people who loved them, and some of them later fought to keep me where I was. I understand why. That loss isn't a stage in my growth, and I won't use it as one.

The second is that I live with what happened every day, and somewhere along the way I learned the difference between accountability and spectacle.

Here's what belongs in this book, and only this: I was there, I didn't stop what I might have tried to stop, and I helped hide it before I told the truth. I've never found a way to make that smaller, and I've stopped trying to. Understanding how a person ends up in that situation, dissociated and years deep into numbing everything he had ever felt, is real, and it matters to this framework. But understanding has never once meant excuse. You'll see that line on nearly every page of the workbook. I learned it here first, and I learned it the hard way. If I let my own story off the hook, the entire framework is a lie. So I don't.

Where it actually began

Prison is a strange place to locate the beginning of something like this, but it's where IdentiNova actually started.

For the first time since I was a child, I was sober and still. I did the work. Fifteen years of it. I sat with a clinician every week. I finally spoke about the abuse I had never told anyone. I earned a GED, then an associate's degree. I helped build a program raising puppies that went on to serve people with disabilities, and raised three of them myself. Any of that would be worth telling. But the thing that became the framework was smaller and stranger than all of it.

Sober, I realized I had no idea who I was.

Most people get to build a self slowly, as kids: they try on versions, keep some, drop others, and shape the thing over years. I never got that. Every identity I had ever had was an emergency construction, built fast under threat: the invisible one, the pleaser, the one who could take anything, the one who felt nothing. Underneath them there was no actual person I had chosen. So there I was, a grown man behind a wall, with nothing real to stand on. And I had to build something. On purpose. From close to nothing.

That's the realization the whole framework rests on. **Identity isn't simply something you are. It's something that gets built. And if it can be built by circumstance, it can be built on purpose.** I had no names for the steps yet. But I was taking them. I was pulling apart beliefs I had swallowed whole as a child. I was looking at things I had hidden even from myself. I was stripping the authority out of conclusions that had been running me since I was eight, and trying to put something I had actually chosen in their place. I was living Imprint through Yield with no idea those words would ever exist.

The pattern in other people

Coming home was its own kind of shock. I had gone in before cell phones and laptops were part of ordinary life; I came out into a world I didn't have the manual for. I spent four months in a program, about a month with my father, and then got my first apartment.

I started showing up at a recovery center, every day and all day, until they asked if I would volunteer. The director there did something almost no one was willing to do at the time. For about a year I was, by a wide margin, the most publicly hated man in my state: parole granted at my twelve-year mark, rallies to keep me locked up, new legislation, a steady run of headlines, a lot of it distorted. He looked past all of it and took the time to find out who I actually was. He made me a recovery coach, put me through the training and certification, and asked me to build a support group for people coming home from incarceration who were also in recovery. I did. It ran for years. Around the same time I went back for my bachelor's degree.

That's also where I first put a name to a thing I had been feeling without understanding it: impostor syndrome. The more I built, the more certain I became that I would be found out. It wasn't about being unqualified. It was the gap between the life I was constructing and the old beliefs still running underneath it: the eight-year-old's conclusions, still on the job. That gap, it turns out, is its own phase of the work.

The next stretch was harder, and I'll keep it plain. The director who had believed in me got cancer and died. The man who replaced him had no interest in me, and eventually called the press to tell them where I lived, where I worked, and where I went to school. Reporters showed up at the center. I declined, reported it to my parole officer, and was told I couldn't go back. I found work at another recovery organization and kept going. And not long after, the state issued me a citation for the very work the headlines had said made me unfit to be free. Somewhere in there came my own cancer: remission, then a recurrence in a different place, then surgery to remove part of my right lung. I kept working and studying straight through it, and took on more than I needed to, partly to prove to myself that I belonged. I graduated with high honors, gave a speech at the ceremony, and later raised over four hundred thousand dollars speaking for the school's nonprofit.

I'm compressing all of that on purpose. The highlight reel isn't the point. The point is what I started to see while it was happening.

I was working in the field, sharing pieces of my story because that was what built trust with the people I served. Then I built and led a peer team, teaching others to work from people's resilience instead of their deficits. And I kept seeing the same architecture I had lived. Abandonment hardening into invisibility. Shame turning into a permanent story about worth. Survival strategies that had long outlived the danger, calcified into *this is just who I am.* I saw it in client after client. I saw it in my own staff. I still saw it in myself. At some point I stopped seeing my story in it and started seeing a structure.

When the path became a framework

After about three years, my mother was diagnosed with stage four lung cancer and stage two bone cancer, and I took significant time away to care for her. When I came back to work, I was put on paid leave for four and a half months and then let go on a pretext. I was angry, and then I wasn't, because the truth was that the place treated peer work as an afterthought rather than the thing it actually is, and leaving cleared the way for what came next.

In the space that opened up, I did the thing the framework is made of, before it was a framework. I studied my own identities. I traced how I had moved through them: how I was shaped, what I concluded, what I had hidden, what I had stripped of its authority, what I had built on purpose, how I had held it under pressure, and who I had become on the other side. And I understood, finally and completely, that identity is malleable, not fixed. Not concrete. Built.

So I took the word itself apart: **I**mprint, **D**econstruct, **E**xpose, **N**ullify, **T**ranscend, **I**nstall, **T**est, **Y**ield. The eight phases weren't invented. They were named. They had been there the whole time, in the order I had walked them.

Then I wrote the workbook.

Lived first, confirmed later

This is also where the research comes in, and it's why this book grounds itself in research the way it does, rather than the way a textbook would.

I want to be honest about the order, because the order is the whole argument. I didn't read John Bowlby and then understand attachment; I lost the people who were supposed to keep me, decided I was the reason, and only years later found a man who had spent his life mapping exactly that. I didn't study trauma and then notice that my body had kept a record of things my mind had tried to drop; I lived that, and later found Bessel van der Kolk and Gabor Maté putting language to it. I didn't learn that identity is malleable from Carol Dweck or Robert Kegan;

I rebuilt mine from almost nothing in a cell, and then found they had already described how that happens.

Every phase of this framework works that way, and the rest of this book will show it, phase by phase: not science handed down from above to validate me, but science I ran straight into, traveling the other direction, on ground I had already crossed on foot. When the person who lived it and the people who studied it arrive at the same place from opposite sides, that convergence is worth more than either one alone. That's the kind of validation this book is after.

Which brings me to the question people raise about me, and that I would rather meet directly than dodge.

I'm not a psychologist or a therapist. I came to this without the clinical training that usually stands behind a method like it. I do hold credentials: I'm a Certified Peer Specialist and a Certified Recovery Coach, I earned a degree, I've spent years in direct practice, and the state that once rallied against me eventually recognized that work. But none of that is a clinical license, and none of it is where the framework came from. The framework came from having to build a self out of almost nothing and paying close attention while I did it.

I've stopped treating that as a smaller qualification than a degree. It's a different one. And for this particular work (understanding how an identity forms, defends itself, collapses, and can be rebuilt on purpose), it may be the necessary one. IdentiNova is built to stand alongside clinical care, not in place of it; the workbook says so plainly, and so do I. But the part no degree could have produced is the part I had to live.

The order

IdentiNova is the focus of everything that follows in this book. My life is only the path it was carried over.

I've told you this much of the path for a single reason: so you know the framework wasn't thought up and then tried out on a life. It was lived, the whole way through, and only then built: by someone who needed it to be true before he ever needed it to be useful to anyone else.

That's the order, and it matters.

Lived first. Named second. Offered last.

PART ONE

Why This Exists

What Identity Really Is

The Lever Underneath the Behavior

✦

A lot of men get sober in prison. Most of them aren't different when they leave.

I watched it happen for fifteen years. Men who hadn't had a drink or a drug in a decade, clean longer than some free people manage in a lifetime, then using again within a day of walking out the gate. Not because they were weak, and not because they didn't mean it. Because the cell never changed them. It just took away their options. The person who walked out was the same person who had walked in, only rested. Hand that person back his old life: the same streets, the same phone numbers, the same hole where a self should be. The behavior comes back, because the behavior was never the thing. It was a symptom of the thing.

I could have been one of those men. I had every reason to be. What made the difference for me wasn't the years of abstinence; abstinence was handed to me by a locked door, and a locked door has never healed anyone. The difference was that I used those years to become someone the old life no longer fit. By the time I left, the drinking and the using weren't being held back by willpower. They were obsolete. They had nothing left to do, because the person who had needed them was gone.

That distinction, between stopping a behavior and dismantling the self that produced it, is the entire reason this framework exists. And it's the first thing I have to make the case for, because if you don't accept it, nothing else in this book will hold.

Behavior is the surface; identity is the system

Here's the claim, stated plainly: **behavior is almost never the real problem. It's the visible end of something that starts much further upstream.**

We spend our whole lives trying to fix ourselves at the level of behavior. Stop drinking. Stop yelling. Stop procrastinating. Stop picking the wrong people. Be more confident, more disciplined, more positive. And it works, for a while, the way holding your breath works: through effort, until the effort runs out. Then the old behavior comes back, and we conclude that the problem is us: that we lack willpower, that we're broken, that we'll always be this way. We almost never consider the other possibility, which is that we were aiming at the wrong target the whole time.

Because underneath every behavior is a belief, and underneath every belief is a conclusion about who you are. That's what identity actually is. Not your personality type. Not the labels you would put on a form. Not your job or your roles or the answers to a quiz. Identity is the accumulated set of conclusions you carry about who you are. *I'm the kind of person who... I'm someone who always... people like me don't...* They operate quietly beneath your choices, deciding far more than you realize what you do.

I traced how those conclusions get built, in my own life, years before I could have named the pattern, and they always formed the same way: **experience, interpretation, belief, pattern, identity.** Something happens. You assign it a meaning. The meaning hardens into a belief. The belief starts producing behavior. And once the behavior has run long enough, it stops feeling like something you do and becomes something you are. The behavior everyone is trying to fix sits at the far end of that chain. The identity sits at the near end, where it all started, and where it's all still being driven from.

This is why you can't out-behave who you think you are. You can suppress a behavior through sheer force, but the identity underneath is still generating it, and an identity is patient. It will wait out your willpower. It will find a new behavior if you take the old one away. Take a man's drink and leave his belief that he is broken and pain is his normal, and he will find another way to prove it: another substance, another fight, another quiet act of self-erasure. The behavior changed. The system that produced it didn't. So the system produces it again.

It was never the event

Look again at how those conclusions form, because one step in that sequence does almost all the work, and it isn't the one people tend to blame. We blame the experience. *Something happened to me, and that's why I'm the way I am.* But the experience is only raw material. Between what happened to you and who you became sits a single quiet step: interpretation, the meaning your mind assigned to the event. That meaning, not the event itself, is what hardens into belief and then into identity. Leave the event exactly as it was and change only the conclusion a person drew from it, and you get a different person. The event walks in the door. The interpretation decides what it means. And the interpretation is where a self is actually made.

Once you see that, something important follows. The experience doesn't have to be dramatic, or even bad, to build a limiting self. It only has to be misread.

I worked with a woman whose story makes this almost too clear. There was nothing harsh about her childhood. Her family was simply a quiet one. When the television was on, she was told to sit still. When the adults were talking and she tried to jump in, she was told that people were speaking and she would have to wait her turn. None of it was cruelty. It was ordinary discipline, the kind of thing a loving family does to teach a child manners, and it went on that way until she grew up and moved out. But her mind, the way every mind does, drew conclusions from it. It decided she wasn't important enough to be part of the conversation. It decided she was too much, too hyper, that her wanting to speak was a problem. It decided everyone else came first. Nobody ever said those things to her. She assembled them herself, out of dinner tables and quiet evenings, and then she became them. She grew into a timid woman who never spoke her mind, who put everyone ahead of herself, who took a back seat in her own life and waited for other people to make her decisions. The household was gentle. The identity it accidentally produced ran her for decades.

Her story is the framework with the trauma taken out, so you can see the mechanism on its own. And it runs the same way even when the experience was a good one. The child praised only ever for achievement, who concludes *I'm only worth what I produce.* The one shielded from every hardship, who concludes *I'm fragile, and the world isn't safe for me.* The kid told constantly how gifted they are, who concludes *if I'm not the best, I'm nothing.* Nothing went wrong in those lives. The praise was real, the protection was loving, the gift was genuine. The mind simply made a meaning out of it that didn't serve the person, and the person spent the next thirty years living inside that meaning.

This is why the framework is for everyone, and I mean that as exactly as I can say it. The one thing every human being shares, whatever their life looked like from the outside, is that they made sense of it as they went, and they've been living inside the sense they made ever since. You don't need a wound to qualify. You don't need a dramatic story. You only need to be a person who once interpreted your life and then quietly became the interpretation. That's all of us.

I draw my own examples from the far end of that range, because that's the life I have to offer as proof, and because a process that holds there, under that kind of weight, will hold anywhere. But don't mistake the severity of my story for the size of the framework. The interpretation is the hinge whether the experience that turned on it was overwhelming or entirely ordinary. What was built can be looked at, and what is looked at can be rebuilt, whether you're dismantling a self forged under fire or one you slipped into across a thousand quiet evenings without ever choosing it.

Why nothing held until I aimed lower

Take a single pattern: this fear, this habit, this cycle you keep repeating. At that level, identity isn't just one factor among many. It's effectively the root. And I'll push hard on that claim, because I didn't read it anywhere. I lived the proof.

I didn't drink because I liked alcohol. I drank because, the first time, it did something no person had ever done for me: it made the heaviness lift, the shame quiet, the constant scanning stop. It made me feel, for an hour, like I belonged somewhere and wasn't the reason people left. The substance wasn't the point. It was the solution to an identity: *I'm broken, I'm too much, I don't belong, pain is just my normal.* For thirty years I tried, in the ways available to me, to manage the behavior. I never once touched the belief underneath it. And so the behavior always won, because I was fighting a branch while the root drank freely.

The fighting was the same. I didn't stop being a man who swung first by deciding to be calmer. The fighting was an expression of a self that had concluded the world was dangerous and the only safety was to be harder than whatever was coming. You can't anger-manage your way out of that. The violence wasn't the disease. It was the fever.

What finally worked, the only thing that ever worked, was going after the root. When I got still enough, sober enough, to ask not *how do I stop doing this* but *who am I, and who do I want to be,* the behaviors started losing their grip on their own. Not because I white-knuckled them into submission, but because I slowly became someone for whom they no longer made sense. You don't have to fight a behavior that has nothing left to protect. That's the strong claim of this whole framework, and I would stake my life on it, because in a real way I already have: **change the behavior and it grows back; change the identity underneath it, and the behavior loses its job.**

What identity can't do

And now I have to be just as honest in the other direction, because a claim that explains everything usually explains nothing, and I've watched too much self-help promise that the right mindset can fix a life. It can't. Identity is the root of a *pattern.* It isn't the root of a *life.* Those are different scales, and pretending otherwise would be a lie I'm not willing to tell you.

I beat cancer twice. No amount of identity work shrinks a tumor. I needed surgeons, and treatment, and part of a lung removed. And the most aligned, intentional, beautifully reconstructed self in the world would have died without them. Biology is real. Brain chemistry is real. There are conditions that no reframing reaches, that require medication and medicine and a level of care this book doesn't provide and would never pretend to.

Circumstance is real, too. For a year, with my home and my workplace handed to the press, an entire state had been given a reason to hate me. And no inner work I did made that stop. Poverty is real. Safety is real. Who happens to be standing around you when you're trying to change is real, and it can make the difference between a new self that takes root and one that gets strangled in the crib. I've sat across from people doing everything right on the inside while the world outside gave them nothing to stand on. Their problem wasn't their identity.

And clinical conditions are real. I spent fifteen years sitting with a clinician every week, doing work I couldn't have done alone, on wounds that needed a trained professional and not a framework. Depression, trauma, addiction as a disease of the body and brain: these aren't character flaws waiting for the right attitude. They're real, and they sometimes need real treatment, full stop.

So at the scale of a whole human life, identity isn't the only lever. It's the *overlooked* one: the piece so many approaches leave out, the missing half that biology and circumstance and treatment can't supply on their own, just as it can't supply what they offer. Anyone who tells you identity is everything is selling something. I'm not.

The most changeable real thing

So if identity isn't the only thing that's real, why build an entire framework around it? Why make it the lever?

Because of all the real things that shape a human life, identity is the one you can actually get your hands on.

You can't always change your biology. You often can't change your circumstances, at least not quickly, and not alone. You can never change what already happened to you. The past is closed. But the conclusions you drew about who all of that made you? Those aren't closed. Those were interpretations, most of them made long ago by a younger version of you, working with far less than you have now, and they can be examined and rebuilt. Identity isn't the only real thing. It's the most *changeable* real thing. And that's exactly why it deserves to be the thing you organize the work around, not because nothing else matters, but because this is the one place where what's real and what's workable actually overlap. It's where leverage meets agency. It's the lever you can reach.

That's the whole bet of this framework. Not that identity explains everything. That identity is the highest-leverage thing you can actually change, and that most people never change it because no one ever showed them it was a thing that *could* be changed. They thought it was just who they were.

I want to be careful here, because I came to all of this from the inside, the hard way, before I had any support for it. Only later did I learn that the science had been saying the same thing for decades: that identity is built rather than fixed, and therefore can be rebuilt; that the way we see ourselves shapes what we become; that adults go on developing and reauthoring who they are across an entire lifetime. I'll lay that out properly a little later, because *how I know this is true* deserves its own full accounting and its own honest method. For now it's enough to say that what I'm about to build this book on isn't just one man's theory. It's a conclusion I reached by living it, and then found waiting for me in the research, again and again.

There's one more thing this claim does, quietly, that matters more than any of the rest. If behavior is produced by identity, and identity was built by experience that you didn't choose, then the people around you start to make sense. So does the person you've been hardest on, which is usually yourself. The drinking makes sense. The walls make sense. The patterns you hate in yourself make sense, as solutions to problems you faced before you had any better tools. **People make sense.** That isn't an excuse, and I'll spend real time later on why understanding and excusing aren't the same thing. But it changes the entire posture of the work: from fixing something broken to understanding something built. And understanding, not contempt, is the only ground anyone has ever rebuilt a self from.

That self was built once without your consent, and it's rebuildable now with it. That's what the rest of this book is about. The eight phases that follow are eight moves on that single lever. Everything else is detail.

How an Identity Gets Built

From a Single Moment to a Whole Self

✦

The last chapter told you that identity is built rather than handed down by nature, and that the meaning you made of your life mattered more than the events themselves. This chapter shows you the actual machinery. I want you to see exactly how a self gets assembled, link by link, because the moment you can see how a thing was built, you can see where it can be taken apart. There's no mystery in here, and that's the point. A framework that asks you to trust it without showing you its engine is asking for faith. I would rather show you the engine.

I didn't learn this from a diagram. I learned it by taking my own identity apart in my hands and finding, to my surprise, that it came apart in pieces, and that the pieces went in an order. The same order, it turned out, every time, in me and in every person I have since sat with. An identity isn't poured in one piece. It's assembled, one stage at a time, and there are five stages.

An experience happens. You interpret it. The interpretation hardens into a belief. The belief drives a pattern of behavior. And the pattern, repeated long enough, becomes an identity. Experience, interpretation, belief, pattern, identity. Let me walk you through each one, with a single life carried all the way through, so you can watch a whole self get built out of almost nothing.

The experience

Picture a boy, eight years old, in a house where the adults aren't steady. Maybe a parent who drinks, or who works three jobs, or who is simply overwhelmed and not really there. One night something needs handling that a child should never have to handle. A younger sibling needs feeding, or a bill needs hiding, or a drunk parent needs getting to bed. And the boy handles it.

That's the experience. By itself, it's just a thing that happened. It carries no built-in meaning. Ten different children could live that exact night and walk away with ten different conclusions. The event is only raw material. What gets made of it is the next stage, and the next stage is where the self begins to fork.

The interpretation

The boy's mind, like every mind, can't leave an experience as raw data. It reaches for meaning, because meaning is how a mind makes the world predictable enough to survive in. So the boy concludes something. He concludes that if he doesn't handle it, no one will. He concludes that needing help is dangerous, because the people who were supposed to help weren't there when he needed them.

None of that is written into the night. He authored it, the way any of us would have, reaching for the explanation that made the most sense of what he could see from where he stood. This is the hinge the last chapter pointed at, and I won't belabor it here, except to say this. The interpretation is a guess. It's a child's best theory about how the world works, formed with a child's information. But it doesn't stay a guess for long.

The belief

Repeat an interpretation enough times, across enough nights, and it stops feeling like a theory and starts feeling like a fact. That's a belief. A belief is an interpretation that has hardened, that's been said to you by your own mind so many times you've stopped hearing it as a claim and started treating it as simply the way things are. The boy no longer thinks he had to handle that one night. He believes he can only count on himself.

That belief is now load-bearing. It isn't about one night anymore. It has generalized into a rule about all nights, all people, all of life. And here's the quiet tragedy of it. The belief was true once, in the house he grew up in. It was an accurate read of a real situation. It just was never meant to be carried out the door and applied to every room he would ever enter for the rest of his life.

The pattern

A belief that strong doesn't sit still. It drives behavior. The boy, and then the man, acts from "I can only count on myself" over and over, until the acting becomes automatic. He never asks for help. He takes on too much and refuses to hand any of it off. He keeps a part of himself back in every relationship, because depending on someone is the one thing his deepest belief forbids.

That's a pattern. It's the belief made visible, the conclusion turned into a thousand small behaviors that no longer require a decision. He doesn't choose self-reliance in the moment any more than you choose to flinch. It has become reflex.

The identity

Run a pattern long enough and it stops feeling like something you do. It becomes something you are. The man no longer experiences his self-reliance as a behavior. He experiences it as his personality. Ask him who he is and he'll tell you, with a certain pride, that he is independent, that he is the strong one, the person who doesn't need anyone.

That's identity. It's the accumulated weight of the patterns, hardened into a sense of self so complete that it feels like it was there from birth. "This is just who I am," he'll say, and he'll mean it. He has forgotten that it was ever assembled at all. He has forgotten the eight-year-old, and the night, and the guess. All that's left is the finished structure, standing where a choice used to be.

The loop that locks it shut

There's one more thing the chain does, and it's the cruelest and most important part, because it's what makes an identity feel like permanent truth instead of an old construction. Once the identity forms, it goes to work manufacturing its own evidence.

The self-reliant man doesn't ask for help, so he never gets to discover that people would have shown up. His silence guarantees he keeps collecting proof that he is on his own. The belief reaches out through the pattern, shapes the world into experiences that confirm it, and feeds those experiences back to the top of the chain as fresh evidence. Experience, interpretation, belief, pattern, identity, and then the identity reaches back and produces the next experience, already bent to agree with it.

That's why these things feel so immovably true. By the time you're grown, your core beliefs about yourself have been confirmed thousands of times, and every one of those confirmations felt like plain objective proof. What you couldn't see, from inside the loop, was that the loop was building the proof to order. The world wasn't telling you who you were. You were instructing the world what to hand back.

Why showing you this matters

I'm not walking you through this to be clever about it. I'm doing it because of what it implies, and what it implies is the most hopeful thing in this book. If a self is built, link by link, by a process you can name, then it can be rebuilt by working that same process. Every link is a place to step in. You can learn to catch an interpretation before it sets. You can take a hardened belief back apart into the guess it always was. You can interrupt a pattern. You can build new ones. You can break the loop by feeding it experiences it wasn't expecting. The chain that built the old self is the same chain you use to build a new one. That's not a slogan. It's just the plain consequence of identity being assembled rather than fixed.

The eight phases of the framework are, underneath all of it, a set of tools for working these links on purpose instead of letting them run on their own. I won't get ahead of myself, because each of those phases has its own chapter waiting. For now it's enough to see the map they act on. The model is the map. The phases are the moves.

I'll be honest that I didn't invent the idea that interpretation hardens into belief and belief drives behavior. The broad shape of it lines up with how cognitive science has described the mind for decades. But I didn't find it in a journal. I found it by reverse-engineering my own collapse, and the meeting point between what I dug up and what the researchers had already documented is a story for a later chapter. Here the point is simpler. This chain isn't a private notion of mine. It's close to the way thinking itself appears to work, which is part of why a framework built on it holds.

✦ There's nothing mystical in any of this, and there are no secrets. A self is an assembly. Assemblies can be taken apart and built again. That's the whole promise, and I won't dress it up with a guarantee it can't keep, because taking apart a structure that has stood for thirty years, defended itself for thirty years, and feels exactly like the floor under your feet is genuinely hard work. It can be done. It isn't easy. Both of those are true, and you deserve to hear both.

And it runs in everyone. The boy in the unsteady house and the child in the gentle one are built by the same five stages. So is the person whose life looked charmed from the outside and the person whose life was a war. The inputs differ wildly. The machine that turns them into a self is the same machine, in all of us. Which leads to something I have come to believe about every person I've ever met, and it's the next thing I have to tell you. If we're all built this way, out of whatever we were handed, then no one's identity is stupid, or broken, or beyond understanding. Every one of them, including yours, including mine, makes complete sense.

People Make Sense

Why No One Is Broken

✦

Before we go any further, I have to set down the one idea that the rest of this book is built on. If you take nothing else from these early chapters, take this one, because the framework doesn't work without it, and most of what comes later will only make sense once it's in place. The idea is simple to say and hard to fully believe. People make sense. I mean it as plainly and as completely as it's possible to mean anything. Every person you have ever met, every person you have ever feared or admired or written off, including the one who has done genuinely terrible things, including the one staring back at you in the mirror on your worst day, makes complete sense once you can see what built them.

I didn't arrive at that as a warm sentiment. I arrived at it as the only conclusion that survived contact with my own life, and then with the lives of hundreds of people I have sat across from since. From the outside, a great many of those lives looked senseless. They looked like bad choices stacked on bad character. But every single time, without one exception I can recall, the senselessness dissolved the moment I could see the chain that produced it. Trace the experiences, the interpretations, the beliefs, the patterns, and the person stops being a puzzle or a disgrace and becomes what they were the whole time: a reasonable result of an unreasonable set of inputs.

What the phrase actually means

It's worth being precise here, because the phrase is easy to mistake for something softer than it is. It doesn't mean people are nice, or that everyone is secretly good, or that if we all hugged it out the world would heal. It means something colder and more useful than that. Given the exact experiences a person was handed, and the interpretations any mind would reach for under those conditions, and the beliefs those interpretations hardened into, the identity that resulted isn't a random defect. It's the logical output of a sensible machine running on the material it was fed. Nobody becomes who they are by accident, or by stupidity, or by some special failing the rest of us were spared. They become who they are by a process that works exactly the same in all of us. Change the inputs and you would have become someone else. The machine would have run the same way.

Understanding isn't excusing

Now I have to draw the most important line in this entire book, because the principle dies the instant this line gets blurred, and a lot of people blur it on purpose. Understanding isn't excusing. Those are two completely different operations, and holding them apart is the whole discipline.

To understand a person is to see the chain of cause that produced them. To excuse a person is to use that chain to lift the responsibility off them for what they do. The first is the beginning of all real change. The second is a trap that prevents it. I can explain, in full and sympathetic detail, how a human being ends up doing the worst thing he'll ever do. I have had to do exactly that with the worst thing I have ever done. And not once, in all the explaining, did the explanation reach down and carry the responsibility off my shoulders, because that's not what understanding is for. Understanding tells you how you got here. It says nothing about whether you get to stay. Cause isn't permission.

The framework needs both halves and refuses to trade one for the other. It needs understanding, because you can't change a self you're at war with and don't comprehend. And it needs accountability, because a change that costs you nothing and asks nothing of you was never a real change to begin with.

What it takes off your back

Once you really take hold of this, something heavy lifts off the work, and it's the very thing that stops most people before they start. It pulls shame out of the engine.

Most attempts to change a person run on shame. Be better. You should be ashamed. What's wrong with you. And shame is a terrible fuel, because shame is only the old verdict wearing a motivational disguise. At bottom it says that something is wrong with you, that you're defective at the core, and a self can't be built on that foundation, because that foundation is the exact thing that has to be torn out. “People make sense” pulls that engine out and drops a different one in. It says nothing is wrong with you that wasn’t a reasonable response to something real. You aren’t a broken thing that needs fixing. You’re a built thing that can be rebuilt. The distance between those two sentences is the distance between work that drains you and work that frees you. You stop spending your strength hating the structure and start spending it on the construction.

The reason it leaves no one out

This is also why the framework has no one it turns away. If every identity is the sensible output of a formation no one chose, then there’s no such thing as a person too broken to understand, or too far gone to rebuild, or too strange for the chain to explain. The principle is what holds the door open to everyone. It doesn’t matter how ordinary or how catastrophic your formation was. It doesn’t matter whether the world has already decided what you are. The same machine that built everyone built you, and what was built can be understood, and what’s understood can be changed. That isn’t a special mercy handed to a deserving few. It’s a description of how all people work, which means it reaches all people, which means it reaches you, whoever you are and whatever you’ve done.

I want to guard this against the easy misreading, because somebody always reaches for it. Saying people make sense isn’t saying anything goes. It’s not a soft world where no one is ever wrong and every act gets a pass because somebody had a hard childhood. You can hold the deepest compassion for how a person came to be the way they are and hold an absolutely hard line on what they do about it from here. Those two things belong together. The clearest-eyed compassion I know is the kind that understands you completely and still expects everything of you. That’s how I try to treat the people I work with, and it’s how I have had to learn to treat myself. Full understanding. No excuses. Both hands.

What it doesn’t promise

I won’t oversell it. Understanding why you’re the way you are is the start of the work, not the finish of it. There are people who understand themselves with perfect clarity and never change a thing, because understanding opens the door, and walking through it is a separate act, and that act is a choice no framework and no book and no person can make for you. “People make sense” doesn’t promise that everyone will change. It promises that everyone can. The distance between can and will is yours to close, and it stays yours, and that isn't the framework failing you. That's the framework respecting you enough to leave the choice where it belongs.

I had to prove it on the hardest case

I didn't reach this principle as a theory. I had to make sense of a man the world had already filed as senseless and beyond saving, and I had to do it without lying to myself about a single thing he had done. The understanding I offer other people isn't something I read in a book. It's the same understanding I had to fight for, against everything I had ever been told about myself, before I could finally turn it inward. I had to make it true in the one life where it was hardest to believe.

✦

So this is the ground the whole framework stands on. Not that you're good, or innocent, or owed a clean slate. Something simpler and sturdier than any of that. You make sense. You always did. The person you became was the reasonable answer to the question your life put to you, and if you don't like the answer, the good news buried in this entire way of seeing is that the question can be asked again, and answered differently, by you.

The rest of this book is about how. But none of the how works until you believe the thing this chapter exists to tell you. You were never broken. You were only ever built, like everyone else, and what gets built can be built again.

Why Change Doesn't Hold

Why the Old Self Keeps Coming Back

✦

You've changed before. That's the part no one says out loud.

Change is real, and you're capable of it. I've never doubted that, because I've done it, and because I've sat with people who did it against longer odds than most will ever face. So I won't spend a paragraph trying to convince you that change is possible. You already know it is, because you've done it too. You changed all the time. I did the same. I would stop, get clean, get serious, put a new version of myself together, and for a while it would hold. A week. A month. Once, a good long stretch. And then, quietly, with no single dramatic moment I could point to afterward, the old self would come back and take the wheel, and I would watch the new one dissolve as though it had never been there at all.

For most of my life I drew the only conclusion that seemed available. Something in me was broken. I lacked whatever other people had. I was the kind of person change didn't stick to. It took me a long time, and more failed attempts than I could count, to understand that I had the diagnosis exactly backwards. The change didn't fail because I was weak. It failed because I kept aiming it at the wrong layer.

Aiming above the thing that was running me

Earlier in Part One I made the case that identity is the lever beneath every behavior. If that's right, it explains something willpower never could. It explains why change slips.

Almost everything we reach for when we want to become different operates a level above identity. It works on the behavior, or the mood, or the thought in front of us, and it can work genuinely well at that level. That's the part worth saying clearly, because I'm not here to tell you the things you tried were worthless. Most of them do real work. But the identity underneath is the thing producing the behavior in the first place, and when it goes untouched, it doesn't fight you. It just waits. And then it quietly rebuilds whatever you tore down, because the blueprint was never edited.

I know that pattern from the inside, because I reached for nearly every tool a person can reach for, and I watched each one do exactly that.

Everything I tried, and what each one couldn't reach

I tried willpower first, the way most people do. Grit my teeth, hold the line by force. And willpower works, for as long as the will holds. That's the catch no one mentions: it's a muscle, and muscles fatigue. I said earlier that an identity will outlast your willpower, and it does, every time, because it never gets tired and you do. The day your attention slips, the old self is still there, fully rested, waiting to take back the wheel. Force was real. It just wasn't durable, because it never touched the thing generating the pull.

I tried geography. New city, new job, leave the old life and the old crowd behind and become someone new somewhere else. There's real wisdom in changing your environment, and I'll say later that the people standing around you matter more than almost anyone admits. But I kept proving the oldest truth about a geographic cure: wherever I went, I had to bring me. The scenery changed. The conclusions I carried about who I was didn't. Within months I had rebuilt the same life with different street names, because I was the one building it, and I hadn't changed.

I tried stopping the behavior head-on. Just quit the thing. And I could, sometimes for a long time. But I had taken away a behavior while leaving the belief it served fully intact, and a belief that still needs expressing will always find a new way out. Take the drink from a man who is certain he is broken and that pain is his normal, and unless something reaches that certainty, he will find another way to prove it. Another substance, another fight, another quiet act of self-erasure. I wasn't failing to stop behaviors. I was succeeding at stopping them and watching the system that produced them simply route around the gap.

I tried motivation. The clean high of deciding, the surge that comes the night you finally resolve that this time will be different. Motivation is a wonderful starter and a terrible engine. It's built to ignite things, not to sustain them, and it fades on its own schedule no matter how sincere you were when it arrived. I mistook the intensity of the feeling for the durability of the change, every time, and every time the feeling went where feelings go, and left the old architecture standing.

And I tried the bright surface of mindset work. Affirmations. Telling myself the better story in the mirror. I want to be careful here, because the instinct behind this one is right: how you see yourself genuinely shapes what you become. But you can't install a new belief by saying a nicer one over the top of the old one while the old one sits underneath, unexamined and fully in charge. Some part of you knows you're performing, and it keeps its own counsel. I'll come back later to why a belief has to be worked all the way down rather than painted over. For now it's enough to say I tried the paint, more than once, and watched it peel inside a week.

The layer underneath

Look at that list and the pattern is hard to miss. Willpower, a change of place, stopping the behavior, the motivational high, the affirmation on the surface. Every one of them operated above the identity layer. Every one could move the thing it was aimed at. And not one of them reached the conclusions about who I was that were generating the whole pattern from below, so the pattern always grew back.

This is the reframe I want to hand you, because it's the one that finally freed me. The methods weren't the failure. They were doing honest work on their own layer, and for plenty of people, on plenty of problems, that layer is exactly where the work needs to happen. The trouble comes when the thing driving you lives one floor down from where you're working. You can renovate the upstairs beautifully and wake to find the same crack running through the wall, because the crack starts in the foundation, and nobody went down there.

That's what almost everything I tried had in common. It skipped the foundation. Not out of negligence, but because reaching identity directly is hard, slow, unglamorous work that doesn't fit into a slogan or a thirty-day challenge, and most approaches were never built to go there. The missing layer isn't a villain. It's just missing.

That includes clinical care, which was never failing to reach my identity. It was doing its own essential job on its own layer, keeping me alive and stable enough that the identity work was even possible. The two belong together.

What this means for the reader I wrote this for

If you're the person I'm most writing to, I want you to take something specific from all of this, and it isn't a small thing.

The times you changed and it didn't hold weren't proof of a flaw in you. You weren't weak, and you weren't lying to yourself about wanting it. You were doing something far more reasonable than that. You were working hard on the layer you had access to, the behavior, the mood, the mindset, while the thing actually steering kept its position underneath, untouched and patient. Of course it came back. It was never addressed. You were solving the right problem at the wrong depth, and no amount of effort at the wrong depth becomes effort at the right one.

That isn't an excuse, and it isn't a soft landing. It's a relocation of the work to the place where it can finally take. People make sense, including the version of you that kept trying and kept watching it slip. You weren't failing to change. You were reaching, again and again, for a layer your tools were never built to touch.

The same floor, found from the outside

I didn't learn any of this from research. I learned it by failing my way down to the foundation over a span of years. Only afterward did I find that people who study change for a living had marked the same floor I had crawled to, coming at it from the opposite direction.

The most rigorous modern work on habits makes the point almost as plainly as I would. James Clear, who has done as much as anyone to show how behavior is built through small repeated actions, arrives at a striking conclusion about why those actions stick or don't: that behavior change which truly lasts is identity change, that the most durable habits are the ones that become evidence for a new sense of who you are, and that aiming at outcomes while leaving identity untouched is why so much habit work quietly unravels. He came to that from the behavior side, studying what makes a habit hold. I came to it from the inside of a life where nothing held until the identity moved. We met on the same floor.

Carol Dweck found a version of it from another angle entirely. Her work on mindset showed that the belief a person holds about whether they can change is itself one of the deepest levers there is, shaping what they attempt and what they become, often from underneath their awareness. That's the part the surface version of mindset work misses. A slogan in the mirror doesn't touch the buried belief about whether you're the kind of person who can change at all, and that buried belief is an identity-level conclusion, not a sentence you can overwrite by repeating a cheerier one. Done at depth, mindset work is identity work. Done on the surface, it's more paint.

I didn't get this from either of them. I worked this out from the inside, across years of watching change slip and finally hold. The researchers arrive at the same conclusion from the opposite direction, through data rather than damage.

Why this comes before the phases

So here's where Part One has brought us. Identity is the lever. It's the layer almost everything else aims above, which is why change so often refuses to hold, and why that refusal was never the indictment of you it felt like. What has been missing isn't effort and not sincerity. What has been missing is a way to reach the foundation on purpose, deliberately, in an order that holds, rather than waiting for a catastrophe to break it open the way mine finally was.

That's the entire reason the eight phases exist, and it's why they're built the way they are. They aren't another method for the upstairs. They're a way down to the layer where change actually takes, and a way to do there, on purpose, what I only ever did by accident and at terrible cost. Before I show you that path, I owe you an account of why I'm the one who drew it, and how I know it leads where I say it does. That's the next stretch of the road.

Carol Dweck to find [illegible] important [illegible] the work [illegible] mindset showed that [illegible] they can change [illegible] the [illegible] attempt [illegible] become [illegible] their [illegible]. [illegible] growth mindset [illegible] the [illegible] whether [illegible] [illegible] patient.

[illegible] watching [illegible] hold [illegible]

[illegible] Before the [illegible]

[illegible] What [illegible] What has been [illegible] [illegible]

[illegible] They are [illegible]

How I Know It's True

Lived First, Confirmed Many Times Over

✦

There's a particular kind of moment when someone hands you a set of words and tells you they're now the truth about you.

Mine came with three of them: post-traumatic stress disorder, severe anxiety, major depressive disorder. They were said by professionals who weren't wrong, who had the training to name what they were looking at, and who were trying to help. I want that understood plainly, because what comes next is easy to misread. The diagnoses were real. They named something that was genuinely happening to me, and the clinical care that came with them was part of what kept me alive.

But a diagnosis arrives as more than information. It arrives as a verdict. And in the silence right after you receive one, there's a fork that almost no one tells you is there. Down one path, the words become your identity. You're now a depressed person, an anxious person, a disordered person, and the rest of your life arranges itself around the label like iron filings around a magnet. Most people take that path, not out of weakness, but because no one ever showed them there was another. The authority spoke. The matter felt closed.

I didn't take it. Not out of some special strength. By then I had a great deal of practice refusing other people's verdicts about who I was. The diagnosis told me what I *had*. I wouldn't let it tell me who I *was*. I did the clinical work, I took it seriously, and I still insisted on authoring what those words were allowed to mean. I chose to control the diagnosis instead of letting it control me.

I start here because underneath, it's the exact question this chapter answers. When someone tells you something is true, about a person or about a framework for changing people, how do you decide whether to believe it? That's the question I had to settle for myself before I would accept any verdict about my own identity, and it's the same question that governs whether you should trust the framework this book is built on. So I'll show you my answer, and you can weigh it for yourself.

What I am, and what I won't claim

Start with the plainest fact about me. I'm not a psychologist, a psychiatrist, or a licensed therapist, and I never trained to be one. I do hold credentials, just not the clinical kind. I'm a Certified Peer Specialist and a Certified Recovery Coach. I earned a degree as an adult, after prison, while beating cancer. And I've spent years in direct practice, sitting with people through the hardest stretches of their lives. But none of that produced this framework. The certifications taught me to do a job. The degree sharpened how I think. IdentiNova came from neither. It came from the years I spent rebuilding a self I had never been allowed to build in the first place, and from the decades before that when I had no self to speak of at all. It isn't the product of what I was taught. It's the product of what I lived.

A trained clinician can describe the architecture of an abandoned child's identity with a precision I'll never match. They know that country from the air, from study. I know it because I was lost in it for thirty years. Those are two different kinds of knowledge, and neither one replaces the other, but the second is the kind this book is made of.

So let me also be clear about what I won't claim. I haven't run a clinical trial on IdentiNova. There's no control group, no peer-reviewed study with my name on it, no randomized data showing that people who use this framework do measurably better than people who don't. It hasn't been validated the way a treatment gets validated, and I won't dress it in the costume of a science I didn't perform. When I lean on research in this book, I'm never telling you that *studies prove my framework works*. That would be a lie, and one lie is all it takes to bring the whole thing down. If the only truth you count is the kind that comes out of a laboratory, this book doesn't have that to give you, and I would rather say so on this page than imply otherwise on the next.

But laboratory proof isn't the only way human beings have ever come to trust that something is true. There's another way, older and in some respects sturdier, and it's the one this framework rests on.

A bridge, not a replacement

Before I show you that other way, I want to settle what this book is and isn't in relation to the people who do clinical work, because it would be easy to misread everything I just said as a knock on them. It isn't.

This framework is a bridge, not a replacement. It's built to stand alongside therapists, peer specialists, and recovery coaches, not to take their place. The clinician brings the trained eye, the diagnosis, the treatment no framework can provide, the care that kept me alive when identity work alone would have buried me. What this brings is the other half: the path drawn from the inside, by someone who walked it, for the person walking it now. Two halves of one work, pointed the same direction. It doesn't compete with professional care. It completes it.

I'm also not the first person to insist that lived experience is a real form of knowledge. For a while I thought I was, and then I learned I had been practicing a recognized discipline without knowing it had a name. It's called peer support, and it rests on the same claim my whole life had taught me: that having lived through addiction or mental-health struggle isn't a disqualification from helping others through it but a distinct kind of expertise, one people often reach for and trust in a way they don't with anyone else. Pat Deegan helped build that ground. Handed a diagnosis she was expected to organize the rest of her life around, she refused to, and spent her career insisting that recovery isn't something done to a person by professionals but something a person reclaims through their own agency and meaning. The one living it is the authority on it, not only its subject. When I found her writing, it wasn't learning. It was recognition.

How people actually come to know things

So here is the other way of knowing. Imagine a dozen people who have never met, who speak different languages, who live in different countries and different centuries, with no possible way to coordinate their stories. And they all, independently, describe the same thing. You wouldn't trust that less for their lack of a shared method. You would trust it more, precisely because they couldn't have copied one another. When independent witnesses with nothing connecting them arrive at the same place, the agreement itself becomes the evidence. The more separate the sources, the stronger the proof.

That principle is the foundation under everything I'm about to tell you. I didn't arrive at this framework by reading the research and applying it. I arrived at it by living it, alone, with no theory and no vocabulary, the hard way, over a lifetime of having to rebuild a self I was never given the chance to build the first time. I drew my own crude map of how identity forms, how it breaks, and how it can be put back together on purpose.

And then, years later, I started finding that map everywhere. Not because I went looking to borrow credibility, but because it kept appearing on its own, in the work of people who had spent careers studying from the outside the very thing I had survived from the inside. They had never heard of me. Most of them had never heard of each other. They came from fields that don't talk to one another and from decades that don't overlap. And they kept landing on the same ground I had already crawled across in the dark.

That convergence is how I know this is true. A life lived from the inside and a body of research built from the outside, meeting in the same place without ever coordinating. Not proof from a laboratory, but something I find harder to dismiss: the same answer confirmed by independent witnesses, again and again, until the agreement got too consistent to be coincidence.

The witnesses who never met

There are roughly seventeen of them across this book, and part of what makes their agreement persuasive is how little they have in common.

Some came from the science of how the earliest bonds build a self. John Bowlby mapping attachment, Dan Siegel showing how relationship literally wires the developing brain. Others came from the study of belief and thought: Aaron Beck and Albert Ellis, who independently discovered that beneath our suffering sit conclusions we never examined. Others came from trauma. Bessel van der Kolk on how the body keeps the score long after the mind moves on, Gabor Maté on how our worst patterns began as ingenious ways to survive pain, Judith Herman on what it actually takes to recover, Stephen Porges on why a nervous system won't release an old pattern until it feels safe. Brené Brown came at it through shame and worthiness, and what dissolves them. Viktor Frankl came at it through a concentration camp and a lifetime of asking how a person survives the unsurvivable through meaning, with Abraham Maslow charting the same human drive to grow rather than merely endure. Carol Dweck and James Clear arrived from opposite ends of one insight: that the self isn't fixed, and that it gets built through what we repeatedly do. Albert Bandura and Angela Duckworth showed how an identity becomes real only when it's lived under pressure. Robert Kegan traced how identity keeps maturing across an entire adult life. And Pat Deegan, whom you just met, insisted from inside the experience that the person living it is the authority on reclaiming it.

Attachment theorists, neuroscientists, cognitive therapists, trauma specialists, a Holocaust survivor, humanistic psychologists, behavior researchers, a developmental theorist, a leader of the peer-recovery movement. Different disciplines. Different decades. No shared agenda, no coordination, in many cases no awareness of one another at all. And every one of them describes a piece of the same architecture: that identity is formed by experience, can be brought into awareness, and can be deliberately rebuilt.

I'll bring them in one or two at a time, in the phases where each belongs, so you can see exactly where their work meets mine. But I wanted you to see them gathered first, because the group is the argument. Any single one of them could be waved away. Seventeen independent witnesses, from that many directions, landing on the same map a man drew from the inside of his own life, is the closest thing to proof I have, and it's sturdier than it sounds.

Why I don't cite like a textbook

This is also why the book doesn't read like an academic paper. That was a choice, not an oversight.

If I dropped formal citations after every claim and wrote in the hedged language of a journal, I would be telling you a lie about where this came from. That format announces a particular order of events: here's the established science, and here's the author applying it. But that's the reverse of what happened. The science didn't come first. My life came first. The research isn't the source of this framework. It's the confirmation of it. To write it the other way around would launder the real origin, a lived life, into borrowed authority, and the borrowing would quietly steal the one thing that makes this book worth reading.

So I point to the researchers the way you would point to a witness who independently backs up your account, not the way you would cite a textbook you're summarizing. And I hold to honest language about what their work does. You'll notice I say this framework is *grounded in*, *consistent with*, and *confirmed by* established research. You won't catch me calling it *clinically proven* or *scientifically validated*, because those words mean something specific that I haven't earned. The distinction is the difference between honesty and salesmanship, and I intend to stay on the honest side of it.

There's a simpler reason too. I didn't write this for a journal. I wrote it for the person in the struggle, the one rebuilding a self at eleven at night with no one watching. That person isn't served by a wall of citations. They're served by the truth, told clearly, by someone who has been where they are.

The other evidence: a life that kept testing it

There's one more thing I can offer, and in some ways it carries the most weight.

A framework tested once isn't worth much. Mine was tested more times, and against more kinds of pressure, than I would wish on anyone. This is the part people sometimes want me to soften, and I won't, because the breadth of it is the whole point. The same architecture, understand what shaped you, examine what you concluded, rebuild on purpose, had to hold through abandonment and through abuse. Through addiction and through fifteen years of incarceration. Through homelessness. Through three psychiatric diagnoses. Through cancer, twice. These aren't variations on one wound. They're radically different kinds of collapse, and a thing that works on only one of them isn't a framework. It's a coincidence.

This is why, when people ask which part of my story the framework came from, the honest answer is all of it. Not the prison alone, not the diagnoses alone, not the abuse alone. The framework exists because I had to rebuild a self that many times, under that many different conditions, and the same process kept working. That isn't a controlled study, and I would never call it one. But it's a kind of evidence no controlled study could ever produce: a life that kept throwing new kinds of collapse at the framework, tests it was never designed for, and a framework that held every time.

And there's one more kind of evidence, one that took me years to recognize for what it was.

For about eight years, before any of this had a name, I was already handing the route to other people without knowing that's what I was doing. It usually started with a question. People who knew where I had been would ask how I made it out, how I had accomplished what I had, how someone with my history landed the roles I landed. To answer honestly, I had to retrace my own steps out loud. And in retracing them, again and again, with people in recovery and people coming home from prison and people simply trying to become someone new, I was walking them down the same path I had walked myself. I didn't know it was a framework. I thought I was just telling the truth about how I had done it.

The ones who actually walked it changed. Not all of them. The ones willing to do the work, the hard and unglamorous work of looking at what shaped them and rebuilding from there, reclaimed something. I watched people take back an identity they had handed over years before to addiction, to a record, to a label, to everyone who had told them who they were. I'm not going to put a number on that, because I never counted and I won't pretend to a precision I don't have. But I saw it happen too many times to call it luck, and I saw it fail to happen every time someone wanted the result without the work, which told me the process was real and not magic.

That's the part that carries the most weight, in the end. The framework proved itself before I was even trying to make it work. It wasn't being tested. It was just being told, truthfully, and it kept producing change anyway. Only later, looking back, did I see that every time I had answered that question, I had been guiding someone through the same eight stages I would one day name.

So here's how I know it's true, stated as plainly as I can. I knew it from the living of it, well before any theory. Seventeen independent thinkers, from fields that never coordinated, confirm its pieces from the outside. A life with more kinds of breakdown in it than most people will ever face kept testing it and kept finding it sound. And for eight years it changed other people's lives before it had a name or a shape, in the hands of someone who didn't yet know he was holding anything. That isn't laboratory proof, and I'll never call it that. But a single life, a crowd of strangers, and years of people I watched reclaim themselves, all reaching the same answer from that many directions, becomes its own kind of certainty. For me, it's enough to trust.

That's the standard I'll hold myself to for the rest of this book. Now I can show you why the eight phases come in the order they do, because a true thing still has to be walked in the right sequence to be of any use to you.

Why Eight Phases, and Why in This Order

The Path Was Walked Before It Was Named

✦

I'll name the suspicion before you have to, because if I were you, I would have it too.

The eight phases of this framework spell a word. Imprint, Deconstruct, Expose, Nullify, Transcend, Install, Test, Yield. The first letters spell IDENTITY. And the moment a reader notices that, a fair and skeptical question arrives: *did he discover eight real stages, or did he just find eight words that fit a tidy acronym?* Because anyone can force a life to spell something. Self-help is full of clever frameworks that are mostly clever and very little framework: the structure exists to be memorable, not because it's true.

I would have the same doubt. So let me tell you exactly how the order came to be, including the part where I doubted it myself.

I didn't start with the word

The sequence came first. The word came last, as a kind of gift I didn't see coming.

For years I wasn't building a framework at all. I was just trying to survive my own life, and then, slowly, to rebuild it. I noticed, first in myself and later in the people I worked with, that the rebuilding always seemed to move through the same stages, in roughly the same order. You had to understand what had shaped you before you could question what you had concluded. You had to question your conclusions before you could see the survival patterns underneath them. You had to see those patterns before you could loosen their grip, and loosen their grip before you could reach for something new, and so on. I was mapping the territory I had crawled across, naming each stretch as I recognized it.

It was only after I had the stages laid out, after the work of identifying them was already done, that I looked at the list and saw what the first letters spelled. Identity. The very thing the whole process was about. I would love to tell you I planned it. I didn't. I had spent my life unable to form an identity, then spent years rebuilding one from nothing, and when I finally wrote down the steps it had taken, they spelled the word for the thing I had been chasing the entire time. It stopped me cold. It felt less like cleverness than like a confirmation I hadn't asked for.

And then I refused to trust it

Here's the part that matters more than the acronym, and the part I would want you to weigh if you're deciding whether to trust me.

I didn't take the spelling as proof. A word forming out of my own list was exactly the kind of thing that should make a careful person suspicious, not satisfied. The neatness of it could just as easily have been a sign that I had unconsciously bent the steps to fit, choosing words because they started with the right letters rather than because they named something real. If the order only worked as a spelling and not as a sequence, the whole thing was a parlor trick, and I would rather have known that than build a book on it.

So I went back and interrogated the order itself, with the acronym set aside. I asked the hard question of every phase: *does this actually have to come where it comes, or could it sit somewhere else?* I tried to break the sequence. I looked for places where you could skip a step, or swap two, or start in the middle, and have it still hold. And what I found, slowly and to my own relief, was that you can't. The order isn't decorative. Each phase depends on the one before it in a way that doesn't survive being rearranged. The acronym got me to look closely. The logic underneath is what made me trust what I saw.

That's the difference between this and a framework built to be memorable. I didn't reason my way to a clever word and then defend it. I lived a sequence, recognized the word it happened to spell, and then did everything I could to prove the sequence wrong before I would let myself believe it was right.

Why the order can't be shuffled

Let me show you what I mean, because the dependencies are the actual argument.

You can't question a belief you can't yet see. That's why understanding what shaped you has to come before examining what you concluded. There's nothing to examine until the conclusions are visible. You can't strip the authority from a survival pattern until you've exposed what it was protecting; pull the pattern out before you understand its job, and you tear away a defense the person may still need, or it simply grows back, because the fear underneath it was never addressed. You can't build a new identity on top of an old one you never dismantled: that's the affirmation trap, the painting-over-rot I refused to build into this framework, and it's why installing the new has to come after releasing the old, not before. And you can't call any new identity yours, not honestly, until it has been tested under the kind of real-world pressure that tells you whether it will hold when it counts.

Each phase makes the next one possible and is made possible by the last. Skip ahead, and you're trying to build on ground you haven't cleared. Most people who try to change themselves and fail aren't failing for lack of effort. They're failing because they started in the middle, reaching for the new self before doing the work that would let it take root. The order isn't a suggestion. It's the difference between change that holds and change that doesn't.

The shape underneath the eight

If eight phases feels like a lot to hold in your head, there's a simpler shape beneath them: three movements that the eight phases carry out in detail.

The first three phases, Imprint, Deconstruct, and Expose, are about **understanding.** Seeing clearly what's actually there: what shaped you, what you concluded from it, and what's been running underneath your awareness. Nothing changes here yet. You're turning on the lights before you rearrange the room.

The middle phases, Nullify and Transcend, are about **releasing and reaching.** Taking the authority away from what no longer deserves it, and turning, for the first time, toward who you actually want to become rather than only away from what hurt you. This is the hinge of the whole process, where you stop excavating the past and start facing forward.

The last three phases, Install, Test, and Yield, are about **building and living.** Making the new identity real through practice, putting it under genuine pressure to find out whether it holds, and finally letting it settle into something you simply are, rather than something you're performing. Understanding, then releasing and reaching, then building and living. That's the journey, in three beats, that the eight phases walk one careful step at a time.

✦

I've spent these foundation chapters making a series of claims: that identity, not behavior, is the lever worth reaching for; that the framework had to come from someone who lived it rather than only studied it; that I know it's true by the convergence of a life and a crowd of independent witnesses; and now, that the path through it runs in a particular order for reasons that don't survive being rearranged.

That's the case for why this exists and why it's built the way it is. What's left is the path itself: the eight phases, one at a time, each one drawn from the part of my life where I learned it and confirmed by the thinkers who found the same ground from the other direction.

We start where the work always starts, and where I started: with what shaped you, before you ever had a say in it.

PART TWO

The Eight Phases

Imprint

What Shaped You, and Why You Couldn't See It

✦

The first time my life went quiet, I didn't recognize the person it left behind.

I was in prison, and I was sober, both for the first time in longer than I could measure. For most of my life something had always been chasing me. A feeling I was outrunning. A substance I was reaching for. A room I was reading for the next threat. Noise stacked on noise, and I had never once been still enough to hear what was underneath it.

Then I was still, because there was nowhere left to run. And in that quiet I went looking for myself and found almost nothing I could call mine. No center I had chosen. No person beneath the survival who felt like me.

What I found instead was a stack of selves I had never decided to become. The one who made himself small so he wouldn't be seen. The one who tried to please his way out of being left. The one who had concluded, far too young to question it, that he was the reason people went away. I didn't build those on purpose. They were built in me, early, under pressure. And by the time I was a grown man sitting in a cell, I had been mistaking them for my personality for thirty years.

That stack has a name. I call it your **imprint**.

Why the framework starts here

An imprint is something laid down in you by experience, before you had a say in it, that you later mistake for your nature. It isn't a memory. You can lose the memory entirely and keep the imprint running at full strength. It's the conclusion the experience left behind, about who you are and what you're worth and what people do, operating underneath your choices like code you never read but run every day.

The reason it runs you so completely is that it doesn't feel like a belief. It feels like the truth. The man who decided at eight that he makes people leave doesn't walk around thinking he holds a belief about himself; he walks around bracing for the door. The conclusion has gone invisible. You can't argue with it because you can't see it: you aren't looking at it, you're looking out *through* it. It isn't in the room with you. It's in your eyes.

That's the problem the whole framework had to solve, and it's why this is the first phase and not a later one. You can't rebuild an identity you can't see. I needed a locked door and a clear head before mine became visible to me. But that isn't a method, it's just how long it took me and what it cost. Most people never get that still. They stay in motion their whole lives, busy and distracted and productive, while the imprints keep running underneath, choosing the partners, picking the fights, whispering *you'll be found out* in the exact moment things start to go well. Unseen, unquestioned, and therefore in charge.

So the framework opens by getting still on purpose: by seeing the architecture deliberately, instead of waiting for a catastrophe to force it into view. And the way it does that is by changing the question.

Most people bring one question to their own struggles: *what's wrong with me?* It feels honest, but it's a trap. It assumes the answer is a flaw, sends you hunting for the broken part, and keeps you standing in judgment of yourself, the one posture from which almost nothing has ever changed. Imprint replaces it with a different question: *what shaped me?* That single swap moves the whole thing from judgment to understanding, from *I'm broken* to *I was formed*, and formation, unlike brokenness, has a history you can actually examine.

Underneath that swap is the conviction the entire framework rests on, the one I'll keep returning to: **people make sense.** Not every pattern is healthy, and not every adaptation should continue, but the overall shape of who you became makes sense given what you lived. The invisible kid makes sense if visibility once meant danger. The over-pleaser makes sense if love once felt like something you could lose. None of it dropped out of the sky. All of it was a solution to something, once. That isn't an excuse. I'll come back to why understanding and excusing aren't the same thing. It's a starting point.

The pattern underneath the patterns

When I finally started tracing my own patterns in that cell, the thing that struck me wasn't any single one of them. It was that they had all been built the same way. Not loosely: the same actual sequence, every time. That sequence became the spine of the whole framework:

Experience → Interpretation → Belief → Pattern → Identity.

Something happens. You assign it a meaning. And the meaning, not the event, is the hinge everything turns on. The meaning hardens into a belief you simply accept as true. The belief starts producing behavior. And once the behavior has run long enough, it stops feeling like something you do and starts feeling like something you are. That's the moment an adaptation finishes disguising itself as a personality.

I could run my own life straight through it and the mystery fell out. The experience: the people I depended on were gone, and I was a child reaching for an explanation. The interpretation: it must be me. The belief: *I'm the reason people leave, and I'm not worth staying for.* The pattern: disappear, please, brace, never need too much. The identity: a quiet, watchful man who called himself "just private" and "just independent" and never once suspected those words were scar tissue.

Seeing the sequence didn't fix anything on its own. But it told me the thing wasn't a life sentence. What gets built in a sequence can be examined one link at a time. And that, link by link, is the work every phase after this one does.

How mine got laid down

That compressed version is true, but it skips what it was like to have those conclusions stamped in one at a time, each one pressing down harder than the last. Let me tell you how mine were really laid down, because the order matters, and because you may recognize the machinery even if your own story looks nothing like mine.

It started with my father. When he left, my whole world broke, and back then we didn't have the language for broken families that people have now. No one sat me down and explained it. So my brain did what a child's brain does with something too big to hold. It replayed the last scene over and over, trying to force it to make sense. But it didn't replay what actually happened. Every time it came back, it came back with my father saying that I was the reason he was leaving. He never said that. I'm almost certain of it. But the real words are gone now, buried under the version my mind built, and that version taught me the first thing I ever believed about myself. I'm the reason people leave.

Then my brother left. I had loved him the way an eight-year-old loves the one person who feels safe, which is to say completely, and probably exhaustingly. I tagged along everywhere he went. I know I was a pain to have around. But a child clings to whatever feels safe, and he was it. By the time he went, the conclusion about my father had already set, so I didn't have to wonder whose fault it was. I already knew. What his leaving added were new verdicts, stacked on the first. That no matter how hard I tried, I would never be good enough to make anyone stay. That loving someone all the way, holding nothing back, was dangerous. That my mother, crying in the next room at night, was crying because of me. What does a child do with all of that except try to disappear. So that's what I did. I started shrinking down inside myself, hoping not to be seen.

And then, while I was already that small, the abuse began, and it carried imprints heavier than anything before them. The man who did it threatened me into silence. He told me it was my fault. He told me I was the one making him do it. And my mind, already trained to believe I was the cause of every bad thing, took the lie without a fight, because it matched what I already knew. So a new verdict set on top of the rest. I wasn't only the boy who made people leave. I was the boy who makes bad things happen. I had broken my family, and now I was making a grown man do this. I want to be as clear as I have ever been about anything in this book. None of that was true. A child can't make an adult abuse him. The fault was his, all of it, every ounce. But a child has no such defense in the moment. I only had the lie, and the lie fit the shape of everything else, so I swallowed it as truth and tried even harder to vanish.

It showed. The school called my mother to tell her something was wrong with me. That I had no friends. That I wouldn't speak or take part in anything. They ran their assessments and sent me to a therapist at the school, and I want to say this part carefully, because it matters for everything this book argues. It didn't help me. It made things worse. Because to a boy already certain he was the broken one, being assessed and handed to a therapist wasn't relief. It was confirmation. Now it was official. Something was wrong with me, and the adults had the paperwork to prove it.

It went further than that. Eventually I was removed from the home, and after I ran away I was placed in a camp for troubled kids. To me that wasn't protection. It was the final proof of the thing I already believed, that I didn't even deserve to be in a family, because I was too broken to belong in one. And when I finally came home, the home I had been so afraid of losing was unbearable to be in. I watched my mother cry at night. The apartment felt hollow. And that hollowness settled onto me like a sentence read aloud, because it was the exact thing my mind had been telling me all along. This emptiness is what you deserve. This is what you made.

That's where I was the day I found alcohol. I won't dress it up into something it wasn't. A child carrying that much, certain he had earned every pound of it, will reach for the first thing that quiets the noise in his head. I found mine early. And for a long while it worked, which is the most dangerous thing a thing like that can do.

I have laid all of that out in a row on purpose. Read straight through, it looks like the assembly of a broken person. But look again at what it actually is. Every line of it is a conclusion. I'm the reason people leave. I'll never be good enough. Loving people is dangerous. I make bad things happen. I'm the broken one. I don't deserve a family. Not one of those is a fact. Every one is a verdict a small boy handed down on himself, with a child's information, under more weight than a child should ever carry, with no one there to tell him he had it wrong. That is what an imprint is. And the only reason I can lay them out now, name them one by one without flinching, is that I finally got still enough to see them for what they were. Not the truth about me. The conclusions I drew. And a conclusion, unlike a fact, can be picked up, turned over, questioned, and in time set down for good.

What I found later, going the other way

I didn't read the science and then understand my life. I understood my life from the inside, alone and sober, with no framework and no vocabulary. Only years later did I run into the people who had mapped the same ground from the other direction. When I found them, it didn't feel like discovering something new. It felt like reading a careful description of a room I had already been locked inside for years.

The first of them was **John Bowlby.** Long before I knew his name, I had concluded that a child's earliest relationships set the terms for everything after. Bowlby spent a career proving it. His work on attachment showed that the bonds we form as children do far more than shape our behavior: they build an internal map of safety, belonging, and worth that we then carry into every room we ever enter. He called these *internal working models:* templates, laid down early, for what we can expect from people and what we believe we deserve from them. In books like *Attachment and Loss* and *A Secure Base,* he described exactly what I had lived without being able to name: that identity begins forming long before we're old enough to consciously participate in it. The emotional imprints of childhood become the scaffolding of the self. That's not a metaphor I borrowed from him. It's a conclusion I reached in a cell and found waiting for me in his pages.

The second was **Dan Siegel,** and he answered a question Bowlby left open: *why do these things feel so permanent?* Siegel's work in what he calls interpersonal neurobiology showed that early emotional experience doesn't just leave a psychological residue: it physically shapes the developing brain, wiring patterns that later feel, from the inside, like bedrock. Like simply *who we are.* In *The Developing Mind* and *Mindsight,* he makes the case that identity is never only psychological. It's neurological, relational, and embodied: built in the brain, between people, and in the body, all at once. When I read him, the strangeness of my own experience finally made sense. Of course the invisible one felt like my nature. It wasn't a thought I could talk myself out of. It had been built into me at the level of wiring, by relationships, before I had any defense against it.

Two men. Different decades, different disciplines, neither one of them anywhere near my life. And both of them describing the cell I was sitting in.

That convergence, the man who lived it and the researchers who studied it arriving at the same place from opposite sides, is worth more than either one alone. The phase earns its place here not because an expert handed it down to me, and not only because I survived it, but because both turned out to be true at once.

Before the rest of the book

You have an imprint too. Everyone does. You didn't choose the earliest version of yourself any more than I chose mine: you adapted, the way children do, to the conditions you were handed. Some of what got built still serves you. Some of it stopped serving you years ago and has been making decisions on your behalf ever since, out of sight.

One thing has to be said before the rest of this means anything, because the whole framework stands or falls on it: **understanding what shaped you isn't the same as excusing it.** Tracing a pattern to its origin doesn't hand you a pass. It hands you the truth, and the truth is what makes responsibility possible in the first place. You can understand exactly where something came from and still decide, fully and accountably, that it doesn't get to lead anymore. That's the only place that decision has ever been made from. Self-contempt has never rebuilt anyone. Clear sight has.

There's no broken part to find here. There's only a person who was shaped, usually under conditions they didn't choose, doing the best they could to survive what was happening. A person who, maybe for the first time, gets still enough to look.

That's where it begins. Not in judgment. In understanding.

Deconstruct

The Beliefs You Never Agreed To

✦

There was a stretch of years when I was running recovery programs, responsible for the work and the people inside it, while my own mind kept insisting I had no business in the room.

By every visible measure it was going well. I had come up through the ranks into leadership, first an assistant program manager, then an assistant director, then a program manager, and I was leading teams and getting recognized for the work. And underneath all of it ran a sentence, quiet and certain, nearly every time I sat at a table I was supposed to belong at: *you don't actually belong here, and any minute now they're going to figure that out.*

It didn't feel like a thought. It felt like a fact I was noticing. Like weather. It never argued its case, because it didn't have to. It had been true for as long as I could remember, and things that have been true your whole life stop sounding like opinions.

Why there's a phase called Deconstruct

It took me years to understand what that sentence actually was, and understanding it is what eventually convinced me the framework needed a phase like this one.

The sentence wasn't a report on my competence. It was a belief: a conclusion I had drawn decades earlier, in another life entirely, and never once stopped to examine. I had carried it out of an eight-year-old's house and into a professional's office, and the only thing that had changed was the costume it wore. The boy who decided he was the reason people left had become a man certain he would be found out. Same verdict. New room.

What I couldn't stop turning over was that the belief was running my inner life in flat contradiction to the evidence. The trust, the results, the recognition:

none of it touched the sentence. The belief simply ignored whatever didn't confirm it. And it could do that, I came to see, for one reason only: I had never made it stand still and be examined. It had survived this long precisely because it had never been questioned.

That was the realization. The thing shaping me wasn't only what had happened to me. The first phase had already taught me that much. It was the *conclusion* I had drawn from what happened: a verdict that had detached from its origin and taken on a life of its own. You could understand everything about what shaped you and still spend your days obeying a sentence you handed yourself when you were too young to know better. The experience and the conclusion were two different layers, and the conclusion needed its own reckoning.

I might have written all this off as my own particular wiring if I hadn't started seeing it everywhere.

When I was building and leading a peer team, working with people in recovery and coming home from incarceration, I watched the same thing play out in person after person. People who had done real work understanding their pasts, who could tell you exactly what had shaped them, and who were still, right in front of me, taking orders from conclusions they had never audited. *I always ruin things. I'm too damaged for this. People like me don't get to have that.* They said it the way you would state your height. Not as wounds. As specifications.

That's when I knew it wasn't just me. The gap between what shaped a person and what that person had concluded was structural. It showed up too reliably, in too many lives, to be anything but a real and separate stage of the work. Understanding the past didn't dismantle the verdict. Someone had to go back and examine the verdict itself. That's the phase I came to call Deconstruct, and that's why it exists.

What it's really claiming

If I had to compress the whole phase into one line, it's this: **the experience was real, but the conclusion you drew from it was optional. And it's the conclusion, not the event, that has been making your decisions ever since.**

Something happened. That part isn't up for debate, and the framework never asks anyone to pretend it was smaller than it was. But the meaning assigned to it was the work of a mind doing its best under hard conditions, usually young and frightened with nothing else to go on. A child who is left doesn't simply experience being left; he explains it to himself, because a mind can't tolerate an event with no meaning. And the explanation a child reaches for is almost always the one that turns the blame inward: *it's me, something about me makes people go.* Strange as it sounds, that version feels safer. If it's about me, maybe I can control it. The alternative, that the people who were supposed to keep you didn't, is more than a child can hold. So he draws the conclusion, and then lives as though it were a law of physics instead of the guess of a scared kid.

I'll admit I was tempted, when I was building this, to make it the encouraging phase, the one where you swap the ugly belief for a beautiful one and feel better by Friday. Most of the self-help I had ever come across worked that way. I didn't build it like that, because my own life had already proven it doesn't hold. You can't argue with a buried belief by shouting a nicer one at it; the old one is still down there, unexamined, and it knows you're performing. Painting an affirmation over a rotten conclusion buys you about a week. So I built the phase to move *toward* the old belief instead of away from it: to examine it honestly, all the way down, until it loses its automatic authority and drops from *the truth about me* back to *a claim I once made and am allowed to question.* That's slower and far less flattering than affirmations. It's also the only version I've ever watched last.

Backward, all the way down

I learned to do this in the same place the last chapter started. A cell. Except by now I wasn't only seeing the old conclusions sitting there. I had started taking them apart.

Here is what that looked like. I was sober, for the first time in longer than I could measure, and a sober breath makes you reflect whether you want to or not. At first the reflection was just the obvious question, the one anyone in that situation asks. How did I get here. But I was there for the worst thing I have ever done, and being sober for the first time in years meant the question wouldn't stay small. It opened backward, past the crime, into the whole of my life.

The flashbacks came first, and my anxiety went through the roof. And then the emptiness came back, the same emptiness I had been running from since I was a boy, the one I had spent years drowning so I wouldn't have to feel it. Feeling it again, stone sober, with nothing left to reach for, was one of the hardest things I have ever sat through. But that emptiness turned out to be the thread. It was the thing connecting all of it, every chapter of my life back to the first one, and once I caught hold of it I couldn't let go. I had to understand it. I had to understand how a person becomes that broken.

So I started pulling, and I pulled in reverse. I didn't start at the beginning, because the beginning was buried too deep to reach straight on. I started at the end, with the last event, and I made myself answer two questions about it. What actually happened. And why. Then I took the answer to that second question and treated it as a new event, and asked the same two questions of it. And again. And again. I worked backward through my own life that way, link by link, each why handing me the next thing to examine, until the trail ran all the way back to a kid drawing his first conclusions about himself.

And only when I saw how it all interlocked did the first imprint actually show itself. I could finally make out the shape of it. I had been doing this because I had believed that. The behavior I had hated in myself wasn't random, and it wasn't evidence that I was broken. It was the downstream end of a belief I had drawn decades earlier. Pull on one and the other moved. The more I unraveled, the more of them I found, sitting under everything, each one wired to a pattern I had spent my life acting out without knowing why.

Then came the part that actually changed me, and it's the part this phase is built around. I started to see that the imprints weren't true. Not one of them. They had been handed to me when I was too young to refuse them, installed without my permission by people and events that had no right to define me, and I had been carrying them ever since as though I had chosen them myself. So I started, for the first time, telling myself the truth instead. That I had been a child with no natural defenses. That a kid can't be the reason the adults around him fall apart. That the drugs and the alcohol were never really the point.

That last one cracked something open. I had always told the story as though I were simply a drunk and an addict, as though the substance were the villain of it. Sober in that cell, I could finally see it straight. I wasn't in love with being high, or being drunk. I was in love with not having to remember, not having to feel, not having to wear the coat of shame I had been wrapped in since I was small. The dependency was real, and I won't pretend it wasn't, because those substances do change the brain and its chemistry, and that grip is its own hard fact. But underneath the chemistry, the thing I was actually addicted to was the numbness. The substance was only ever the way I bought it.

And once I was telling the truth, more imprints surfaced that I had never looked at head-on. The biggest was this. That I had to be tough. That the only safe move in a dangerous world was to strike before I was struck, to hurt first so I couldn't be hurt, to get my guard up against everyone before any of them got the chance to leave or to harm me the way the others had. That belief didn't stay in my head. It was where the fighting came from. It was where the petty crimes came from. It was a frightened boy's survival rule still running in a grown man who had long outgrown the danger, and it had helped carry me straight to that cell.

When I saw it all laid out like that, interlocked and traceable, every piece of it tied to a conclusion a child had drawn and never questioned, something settled in me. It made sense. I made sense. And the moment a thing makes sense is the moment you can finally take it apart on purpose. So that's what I did. I started, deliberately, one belief at a time, to deconstruct all of it.

What I found waiting for me

I was doing this work long before I had names for it: years of it sitting with a clinician, dragging old conclusions into the light and learning, slowly, that they were conclusions and not facts. Only later did I find that two men had mapped this terrain with a precision I never could, and had been right about it for decades.

Aaron Beck noticed, working with people in genuine distress, that beneath the surface ran a layer of beliefs about the self, about others, about the world. People simply accepted them as true without ever examining them. They were rarely chosen. They were absorbed early and then defended automatically, coloring everything a person saw. His hopeful discovery was that once such a belief is brought into awareness and tested against reality, it loses its power to run a person from the dark. That's, in large part, the engine of cognitive therapy. It was also a careful description of something I had already been living. Not something I learned from him.

Albert Ellis gave me the piece I had felt but couldn't say: that it isn't the events of our lives that decide how we suffer, but the beliefs we hold about them.

The belief sits between what happens and how we respond, and it's the belief, not the event, that does the deciding. He spent a career showing that many of these beliefs are rigid and irrational, the relentless *shoulds* and *musts* we never agreed to, and that they can be disputed and loosened. They aren't life sentences.

When I came across the bones of Ellis's model, I recognized it on sight, because I had drawn nearly the same line myself. The map I had made of my own formation ran *experience, interpretation, belief*: the meaning in the middle, deciding everything downstream. His ran *activating event, belief, consequence.* Different words. Same machine. I hadn't taken it from him. I had arrived at it from the inside, the hard way, and found him already standing there, having come at it from the other direction.

That convergence is why this phase belongs in the framework at all. Not because Beck and Ellis told me it was true, but because I lived it, reached the same place they had, and only then learned they had been there all along.

✦

There's one thing I had to learn here that I'll pass on, because the phase is easy to misread.

Questioning a conclusion isn't the same as denying what happened. The hardest lesson of this work, for me, was that I could overturn the verdict without dishonoring the history. The leaving happened. The losses happened. What I was questioning was never whether they happened. It was the sentence I had handed myself afterward, the one that said the events meant something permanent and damning about who I was. The event was true. The verdict was a guess. And I was finally old enough, and still enough, to look again.

The first phase showed me what shaped me. This one let me decide what I would go on believing about it, which turned out to be a different thing entirely, and a freer one.

Expose

On Being Seen

✦

For about a year, I was the most publicly hated man in my state.

Parole was granted at my twelve-year mark, and the response wasn't quiet. There were rallies to keep me locked up. There was new legislation. There was a steady run of headlines, much of it distorted, and for a stretch my name belonged to anyone who wanted to use it. Later, a man who had no interest in seeing me succeed called the press and told them where I lived, where I worked, and where I went to school. There's a particular kind of nakedness in that, in having your home and your livelihood and your place of study handed to people who have already decided what you are. I was seen by an entire state, at what they were told was my worst, and what they saw, they hated.

I had spent my whole life certain that this exact thing would end me.

Not the rallies, specifically. The being seen. Somewhere very early, after the abuse, I had concluded that if anyone ever really looked at me they would know, and that knowing would be the end. So I had spent decades becoming unseeable. I took up less space. I needed less. I disappeared inside rooms I was standing in. The deepest law I lived by, the one I never said out loud because I never knew I held it, was simple: be seen and be destroyed. And now here was the nightmare itself, arriving at a scale I could never have built on my own. The whole world looking. The whole world disapproving.

And I was still standing.

That's the strange thing I have to report, and I want to be careful about how I report it. Being publicly hated isn't a gift. It was brutal, it was unchosen, and I wouldn't wish it on anyone or hold it up as a path. It didn't heal me. But it did break something, because it ran the experiment my entire identity had been organized to prevent, and the result came back wrong. I had been fully exposed, looked at by thousands of people at my supposed worst, and the thing I had been certain would annihilate me hadn't. The belief that visibility equals annihilation couldn't survive the plain evidence that I had been about as visible as a person can be, and had lived.

How I stayed standing

The forced exposure had actually started while I was still inside, but in there it cost me little, because by then I had built a good name in that place and most of the recoil couldn't reach me behind the wall. The hard part was getting released into the middle of it. I walked out into a society that hadn't stood still while I was gone, a world that had become a more technical and unfamiliar place than the one I left, and I had to learn to move through it while a media story about me was still running. Trying to rebuild a life and stay low at the same time, with a camera never quite out of frame, was exhausting in a way I don't have a clean word for.

But there was one thing I never lost hold of through any of it. I wasn't the man they said I was, and I knew it. I understood the fear and the sensationalism for what they were, because fear sells in the press and truth doesn't. Not once did the coverage mention the programs I had completed, the education I had chased down inside, or the years of deliberate work I had put into changing who I was, and that absence wasn't an accident. That's simply not how fear works. If they had shown all of it, the change and the effort and the result, the only thing they would have proven is that the system can actually work for a person willing to admit that change is needed, and that was never the story they were selling.

I stayed standing because falling wasn't an option I was willing to take. I had built a new version of myself, and that version doesn't hand anyone else the pen to write my story. I say who I am with my words and my actions, and I had earned my release rather than been handed it. The death threats came, and they were uncomfortable, but most of them came from people with no name and no face beside the words, hiding behind a screen, and threats like that landed empty. Some of the harassment came from police, and I wasn't going to let anyone push me out of a life I was legally entitled to live, so I filed my complaints with internal affairs and kept going. Watchful eyes, suspicion, none of it moved me. I kept showing up. And eventually the whole thing died down, the headlines and the comments and the threats, all of it, because the story ran out of narrative and the spectacle people had been promised never arrived.

What survives only in the dark

The forced version proved I could survive being seen. It didn't set me free. What set me free was the other kind of exposure, the kind I chose.

Years earlier, in a cell, getting still for the first time in my life, I said something out loud that I had never told a living soul. I told a clinician about the abuse. I was a grown man, decades past the thing itself, and I had carried it in complete silence the entire time, certain that speaking it would finally confirm the verdict I had handed myself as a boy: that I was the reason it happened, that something in me had drawn it, that to be known was to be finished.

I said it, and the annihilation I had braced for my whole life didn't come. The clinician didn't recoil. She didn't look at me the way I had spent decades certain anyone who knew would. But what happened next was more complicated than relief, and smoothing it over would betray the very thing this phase is about.

Speaking it cracked something open. The feeling I had spent a lifetime outrunning arrived all at once. Flashbacks came, vivid and uninvited, the past forcing its way into the present faster than I could brace for it. My body did things I couldn't direct. For a while I developed a tremor, a shaking I couldn't still, the body giving its own testimony to what the mouth had only just begun to say. It was, to put it plainly, an enormous amount to carry, and none of it resolved in that first session, or the tenth. Bringing the hidden thing into the light didn't make it gentle. It made it real, and real was hard.

What carried me through that wasn't a framework. It was her. With a trained and steady witness beside me, week after week, I could stay with what had surfaced instead of slamming the lid back down, which is what I had done my whole life. Slowly, the unspeakable became something I could look at, then something I could say, and finally something I could act on. With her support, I came forward and made an official report to the authorities. The thing I had hidden since I was eight, I named, out loud and on the record, by my own choice. That's the farthest distance I've ever traveled from the unseeable boy who was certain that being known would end him.

The clinician was a trained witness, someone whose work was to receive hard things without flinching. The higher test came with people who had signed up for none of that. My own family.

One evening, several of them came to visit me. I hadn't gone in planning to tell them anything. But the conversation drifted, the way those visits do, toward the wreckage of my life, and somewhere in it I realized I needed to clear the air. They deserved to know why things had gone the way they had.

There was a reason that mattered more than my own relief. Some of the people in that room had been quietly blaming themselves for what I had done, carrying a guilt that belonged to none of them, and I couldn't stand to watch it. So I said the first part plainly, with nothing soft around it. My actions were mine. I owned every one of them, fully, and nothing in my past changed that or excused it. But for them to set down a blame that was never theirs to carry, they needed the rest of the story. They needed to understand what had broken me. So I walked them through it. I told them I had been living the only way I had ever known how, because the things that happened to me had quietly stripped away chances other people get to take for granted. I told the truth, all of it, and I kept my head up while I did. And when some of them began to cry, I was the one holding them up.

When I got back to my cell that night, the whole visit ran through my head on a loop. Not because something had gone wrong. Nothing had. And not because the old weight had come crashing back down on me. It was the opposite. It ran on a loop because I had come through it whole. My world hadn't collapsed, the way I had been certain my entire life that it would the instant anyone truly knew me, and I lay there wanting to understand why.

Part of the answer had been in the room with me. At one point during the visit I had watched relief move across my mother's face. Years of self-blame loosening their grip, right in front of me, because she could finally see something I had hidden from her for most of my life. I had been carrying secrets so deep that she had never had a chance to understand what I was going through. And you can't help someone when you don't know what's happening to them. My silence had never protected anyone. All it had ever done was leave the people who loved me holding a blame that was never theirs, in the dark, unable to reach me. Bringing it into the light didn't only free me. It freed them.

That's the phase I came to call Expose, and that's what it does. It brings into the light the things that have been running you from the dark. The survival patterns you've never looked straight at. The secrets you've kept so well that you've hidden them even from yourself. These things don't survive on their own strength. They survive on concealment. Secrecy is their oxygen, and the moment they're seen, by you first and then by someone safe, they start to starve.

This is why the phase sits where it does. Imprint showed you what shaped you. Deconstruct let you question the conclusions you drew. But underneath those conclusions sit the things they were built to hide, the patterns and the secrets the whole structure exists to keep out of view, and you can't loosen the grip of something you won't look at. You have to expose it before you can do anything with it. Naming what shaped you and questioning what you concluded still leaves the hidden thing hidden. Expose is where you finally turn on the light.

One word here has to be exact, because the wrong reading would turn it dangerous. Exposure here doesn't mean exposure to harm. It isn't throwing yourself open to people who will use what they see against you, and it's emphatically not the thing that was done to me by a hostile public. It's the opposite of that. It's chosen. You decide what to bring into the light, and when, and to whom. The exposure that heals is the one you author, on your terms, in conditions you control, witnessed by someone who has earned the right to see it. Where the old exposure was done to me, this one I do. That difference is the entire difference, and it's where the agency that the rest of this framework hands back to you first becomes real.

It also means this is a fair place to say something plainly about doing this work safely. Bringing what's hidden into the light can stir up more than you expect. Old feeling surfaces, sometimes with real force, and you deserve to know that going in. That doesn't mean you need a professional in order to begin. This is your work, and you're capable of doing it. It does mean it's wise to have some support available in case something heavy comes up, whether that's a therapist or a coach, or simply a person you trust enough to sit with you in it. The first time I spoke the unspeakable, it was to a clinician, and that mattered to me. But the point was never the credential of the witness. It's that you don't have to be alone with the hardest things if they arrive. Support here is a safety net, not a requirement, and the work itself is always yours.

What shame can't survive

I didn't read about any of this and then apply it. I lived it, in a cell and on the front page, and only afterward found the people who had mapped from the outside exactly what the exposure had taught me from within.

The closest of them is Brené Brown. Her research into shame lands on a conclusion I had arrived at the hard way: that shame depends on three things to survive, secrecy, silence, and judgment, and that it can't withstand being spoken to someone who meets it with empathy instead of recoil. Shame grows in the dark and dies in the light. She built that from listening to thousands of people tell her the things they were most certain they could never say. I built it from being forced into a light I never asked for, and then, separately, from choosing to speak the one thing I had buried deepest, and discovering in both cases that exposure didn't destroy what I was sure it would. She gave language to the mechanism I had only felt: that being truly seen, and not abandoned in the seeing, is what takes shame, and anything else we hide, apart.

Bessel van der Kolk explains why the thing stays so stubbornly buried in the first place. His work shows that what can't be looked at or spoken doesn't simply fade. It lodges in the body and keeps running underground, the body keeping its score long after the mind has tried to move on, until the experience can finally be faced and put into words under conditions safe enough to allow it. The silence isn't neutral. It's load-bearing. That's why exposure isn't optional housekeeping but the actual mechanism of release, and why doing it safely matters as much as doing it at all.

Gabor Maté adds the posture the whole phase requires. His work on pain and the patterns we build to escape it insists that what we're most tempted to condemn in ourselves began as a way to survive something, and that it's met not with judgment but with honest, compassionate attention to the hurt underneath. That's the spirit Expose has to be done in. You aren't dragging the hidden thing into the light to put it on trial. You're bringing it into the light to understand it, because the same truth that anchors this entire framework holds here too: people make sense, and the thing you hid made sense as a way to survive what you couldn't yet face.

None of this came to me from the three of them. None of this reached me through a book. I had been broken open and stitched back together long before I encountered their names, and their work only corroborates, with the weight of research, what the exposure itself had taught me.

What the light makes possible

There's a reason this phase comes before the ones that build anything new. You can't take authority away from a pattern you've never let yourself see, and you can't rebuild on top of a foundation you're still pretending isn't there. Light first. Everything constructive comes after.

So Expose ends with the hidden thing finally in view, seen by you, and ideally spoken once to someone safe, no longer ruling from a place you refused to look. That isn't the same as being healed of it. It's something more basic and more necessary. It's the thing made visible, which means it can at last be worked with rather than merely obeyed. The pattern is out in the open now. In the next phase, with it finally in the light, you take its authority away.

[illegible]

[illegible]

[illegible]

Nullify

When the Danger Has Passed but the Body Hasn't

✦

By the time I had been sober and still for a while, I was, by any honest measure, safer than I had been in my entire life.

There's a grim irony in where that safety finally arrived. The cell was structured and predictable. Nothing was chasing me. There were no substances pulling at me, no street to survive, no chaos I had to stay three steps ahead of. For the first time in as long as I could remember, the immediate dangers that had organized my days simply weren't there. And my body didn't believe a word of it.

It kept scanning. I read every room for the next threat. I braced at a slammed door, a shift in someone's tone, a footstep with the wrong rhythm, and the whole system would light up as though the old danger had walked back in. The vigilance that had kept me alive through the abuse, through the years on the street, through every place a person learns to watch the exits, wouldn't stand down just because the threat had. I could tell myself I wasn't in danger. I could know it, clearly, in the front of my mind. It changed nothing. The pattern didn't take orders from my reasoning. It answered to something older and lower than thought, and that something was still certain the war was on.

By then I had already done real work on it. I had traced where the vigilance came from. I had questioned the conclusions feeding it. I had even brought it into the light and named it for what it was. And still it ran me, on schedule, every day. That's the hard discovery this phase is built around. Seeing a pattern clearly doesn't retire it. Knowing its origin doesn't strip its power. The pattern keeps its authority long after you've understood it, and understanding isn't the same as release.

Why you can't just rip it out

The obvious move, the one I tried, is to attack the pattern directly. Decide it's the enemy and force it out. White-knuckle it into silence. It doesn't work, and the framework is built around knowing why it doesn't.

A survival pattern is a defense, and it's still standing guard over a fear you haven't yet made safe. Tear it out by force and one of two things happens. Either you've stripped away a defense you actually still needed, and you're left raw in a way you can't handle, or, far more often, it simply grows back, because the fear underneath it was never addressed and the body still believes it requires protecting. This is why this phase can't come earlier. You have to expose what the pattern was guarding before you can safely take the pattern away, or you're pulling out the wires without knowing which ones are load-bearing.

So the first move of Nullify isn't attack. It's the opposite, and it surprised me when I understood it. The vigilance was never my enemy. It kept me alive. The scanning, the bracing, the making myself small, the numbing of everything I felt, every one of them was a real solution to a real danger, back when the danger was real. People make sense, and so do their defenses. You don't take a pattern's authority away by hating it. You take it away by recognizing what it did for you, honoring that it did its job, and then letting it know the job is finally over.

And a survival pattern doesn't have to be born in anything as dramatic as a cell or a war. Most aren't. The perfectionism that started as a way to stay safe from criticism. The people-pleasing that once kept a household calm. The humor that deflects attention before anyone can land a real blow. The habit of needing no one, of staying small, of keeping an exit in view. These are survival patterns too, built to guard against fears that were real at the time, and they run a person just as reliably as mine ran me. Mine were forged under extreme heat, which makes them easy to point at. Yours may be quieter, harder to even recognize as protection. The mechanism is the same, and so is the way out.

Because that's the actual situation. The danger the pattern was built for has passed. The body just doesn't know it yet. And a body isn't persuaded by argument. It's persuaded by evidence, gathered slowly, that it's safe now. That's what nullifying a pattern really is: not commanding the defense to drop, but giving the nervous system enough repeated proof that the threat is gone that it finally, on its own terms, stands down. The authority leaves the pattern not when you order it to, but when the body stops needing the guard.

I want to be honest about how that actually went, because the clean version would be a lie, and a lie here would cost the reader something. It was slow, and it wasn't a straight line. There were stretches where the scanning quieted and I let myself believe it was done, and then a hard week would come, a genuine stress, and the whole old apparatus would roar back at full volume, and I would be certain I had made no progress at all. That despair was its own kind of setback, the belief that the return of the pattern meant the work had failed. It hadn't failed. That's simply how a nervous system releases something: unevenly, circling back, testing whether the safety will hold this time, retreating when it isn't sure. The flare-ups weren't the pattern winning. They were the pattern checking. Learning to read them that way, as checking rather than losing, was a large part of what let me keep going through them.

The verdicts that finally let go

The vigilance was a survival pattern, a thing my body did on its own. But the same authority, and the same slow loss of it, showed up just as plainly in the verdicts my mind had spent a lifetime treating as facts. Those didn't come apart through argument either. They came apart when life finally handed my body evidence it couldn't talk its way out of. Two of them let go in ways I can still point to.

The one that had ruled me longest was the verdict that to be seen was to be destroyed. In the last phase I brought the thing it guarded, the abuse, into the light. What I want to tell you here is what happened to the verdict afterward, because exposure and release aren't the same event.

The day it actually broke its hold was the day I sat down with the authorities and told them, in detail, what had been done to me as a child. I couldn't have chosen a less safe room for it. These were the same people who had arrested me and sent me to prison, who had every reason in their files to see me as nothing more than the worst thing I had done. The whole time I spoke, the old verdict was screaming its forecast at me. They're going to dismiss you. They're going to look at you differently. This is the moment the floor gives way.

None of it gave way. They took me seriously. Their investigation went on to confirm every word I had given them. And a thing I had carried my entire life quietly lost its grip, because I had just been seen, all the way down, in the least safe place I could have picked, and I hadn't been destroyed. That is the kind of proof a body can't un-know. A verdict can survive a thousand arguments. It can't survive evidence like that. That is the reason that, when the public year came and an entire state was handed a reason to hate me, I could stand in it. The verdict that would once have flattened me had already lost its authority. The noise was real, but it no longer had anything inside me to play on.

The second verdict took longer, and it taught me how the authority actually drains out. It was the oldest one of all, I'll never be good enough, except by now it had learned to wear a work costume.

It had stayed quiet for years while I worked as a peer specialist and a recovery coach, because in those rooms my lived experience was the whole qualification and the verdict had nothing to grab onto. It first spoke up when I went back to school, and then a cancer diagnosis and the treatment that followed took the whole of my attention and it couldn't keep its footing. It came back at full strength when I moved into leadership, first as an assistant program manager, then an assistant director, then a program manager. Now the costume fit. You don't have the credentials. You don't belong at this table. Any day now they'll see you're faking and put you out. And my oldest reflex answered the way it always had. I shrank.

What began to change it was learning to recognize the voice. This wasn't a report on my competence. It was the eight-year-old's verdict sitting in a manager's chair. So I started to push back. At one point, running a program, I told my supervisor plainly that impostor feelings paid me visits. Not so I would be rescued from them, but because I was laying out my whole story, lived experience and all, and why it made me the right person for that job, and I wanted it clear that I knew exactly where the feeling came from.

But the thing that finally took its authority was locating the trigger. The verdict fired hardest in rooms full of clinicians, the moment the clinical language started moving. One day I traced why. A room like that dropped me straight back to being the boy the school had sent to a clinician because there was supposedly something wrong with him. The same kind of room, decades apart, and my body had been answering the second one as though it were the first. It was the exact imprint laid down at the very start of all this, the school, the clinician, the certainty that I was the broken one, still firing on schedule in a grown man at a conference table.

The instant I saw that, I could see where I actually stood. I wasn't the broken child being assessed. I wasn't in that room to be fixed. I was in it to help the people we served get through a system I had already gotten myself through. Different room. Different reason. Once I could hold that clearly, the trigger had nothing left to pull, and the verdict lost its grip.

I'll give you one small picture of what it looks like to live once a verdict like that is genuinely gone, and then I'll leave it there. By the time I met the woman I would marry, this work was behind me, and I knew it by what I was able to do. On the day we met, we talked for six hours, and somewhere in those hours I told her all of it. The prison. The crime. The addiction. Everything. Not as a confession, and not as a test of her. I told her because I was drawn to her, and I wanted her to be able to decide, with the whole truth in front of her, whether she wanted to date a man who carried a history like mine.

The old verdict would never have allowed that. To be seen is to be destroyed would have had me hiding the worst of it for as long as I could manage, certain the truth was the very thing that would end us before we began. But it wasn't at the controls anymore. I could let myself be fully known by the one person whose answer I most wanted, and stay standing while she made up her mind. She decided to stay, and in staying she proved one more time what that room with the authorities had shown me first. Being known had stopped being dangerous.

Why the body keeps its guard up

I came to all of this in a cell, by living inside a body that wouldn't calm down no matter what my mind understood. Only later did I find the people who had mapped, from the outside, the exact terrain I had been crawling across.

Stephen Porges gave the clearest account of why my body behaved the way it did. His work describes how the nervous system is constantly scanning, beneath conscious awareness, for cues of safety and cues of danger, and how it won't let go of a protective state until it actually registers that it's safe. You can't think your way out of that. You can't argue a body down from its guard. You have to signal safety to it, again and again, until it believes you. That's precisely what the cell had been teaching me the hard way: the vigilance was answering to safety, not to logic, and it would only release when something deeper than my reasoning was convinced the threat was gone.

Judith Herman mapped the larger shape of it. Her work on recovery lays out that healing moves in stages, and that the first of them, the ground everything else has to stand on, is the establishment of safety. It can't be skipped, it can't be rushed, and the person doing the recovering has to be in control of the pace. That confirmed two things I had learned by failing to do otherwise: that there was no building a new self on top of a body that still felt under siege, and that trying to force the timeline only sent the whole system back into defense.

None of this came to me from either of them. I came to all of this the long way, through my own body, years before I could have pointed to the science behind it. The research simply states in clean terms what my nervous system had long since stopped arguing about.

There's a reason this is one of the places I say plainly that the work often needs company. Establishing safety is frequently not a solo job. For a great many people it involves a therapist, sometimes the right medication, a stable environment, a relationship that proves reliable over time. For me, the steadiness of a clinician and the structure around me were part of what finally signaled to my body that it could lower its guard. This phase asks the nervous system to trust that the danger is over, and trust is far easier to build with a safe other in the room. It's a fair place to bring in professional support, and no failing to need it.

What's left when the guard comes down

When a pattern finally loses its authority, it doesn't disappear, and expecting it to vanish only sets you up to feel defeated when it shows its face again. The vigilance still visits me. The difference is that it no longer runs the place. It's lost its automatic right to decide what I do. It makes a suggestion now instead of giving an order, and I get to answer.

What that leaves behind is strange at first. Space. Room that isn't already occupied by a defense. For someone who has spent a lifetime with every inch of themselves assigned to guarding against something, an unguarded space doesn't feel like freedom right away. It feels unfamiliar, even uncomfortable, like a muscle that finally unclenches and aches in the letting go. But it's the first genuinely open ground you've had, and open ground is the only place anything new can be built.

That's also the boundary of this phase, and I want to honor it rather than rush past it. Nullify only does half the work. It releases the old. It takes authority away from what was hurting you and hands you back the room that authority was holding. It doesn't yet tell you what to put there. Letting go of who you were isn't the same as becoming who you want to be, and the turn from one to the other is its own distinct move. With the guard finally down and the space finally open, the next phase is where you stop facing away from what hurt you and turn, maybe for the first time in your life, toward who you actually want to become. That's Transcend.

Transcend

When Surviving Stops Being the Goal

✦

There came a point, years into my sentence, when I caught myself doing something I had never done before. I was thinking about who I wanted to become.

That sounds ordinary. For me it was almost unrecognizable. For most of my life the entire horizon had been survival. Get through the day. Make the pain stop. Stay one step ahead of whatever was coming. Every identity I had ever built was built for that, to get me out of something, to keep me from being destroyed. I had spent decades running, and a person who is running only ever looks in one direction, backward, at the thing chasing him. It had genuinely never occurred to me to turn the other way and ask what I might be running toward.

The previous phase had cleared the ground for that question. Once the old patterns lost their authority, once my body finally believed the danger had passed, there was suddenly room that had never existed before. And I discovered something I didn't expect about that room. Empty space doesn't stay empty. If you clear out the old identity and put nothing in its place, you don't get freedom. You get a vacuum, and a vacuum pulls. The old self, even stripped of its authority, is still the most familiar thing you own, and in the absence of anything else it will drift right back in to fill the space, not because it rules you anymore, but simply because nothing else is there yet.

So releasing the old turned out to be only half of a single motion. The other half was reaching for something to become. That reach is this phase.

From away to toward

For most of my life, every move I made was a move away. Away from pain, away from danger, away from the version of me I couldn't stand. That's how survival works, and there's no shame in it. When you're in danger, getting away is the only intelligent thing to do. But a life organized entirely around getting away has a hidden ceiling, and I lived under it for decades without seeing it. You can spend your whole existence successfully avoiding what you fear and still never once move toward anything you want. You can get very good at not being destroyed and still have no idea what you're for.

Transcend is the turn from away to toward. It's the moment you stop defining yourself by what you're escaping and start defining yourself by what you're reaching for. The word matters to me. To transcend something isn't to deny it or pretend it didn't happen. It's to rise above it, to stand on top of everything that shaped you and use it as ground rather than be buried under it. The abuse, the addiction, the years I lost, none of it gets erased in this phase. It gets transcended. It becomes the floor I stand on to reach for something higher, instead of the ceiling I keep slamming into.

This is the first phase that builds rather than releases, and that's why it sits exactly here. You can't reach toward a new self while the old one still has its hands on the wheel, which is why everything before this had to come first. But you also can't stop at release, because release alone just leaves the vacuum. The work has to turn, at some point, from tearing down to reaching up. This is where it turns.

Why the turn is so hard

I want to be honest about how disorienting this was, because no one warned me and I think you deserve the warning.

When you've spent your entire life running from things, you become an expert in what you don't want and a complete stranger to what you do. Ask a person who has only ever survived what they want to become, and very often they go blank. I did. The question felt almost offensive at first, like a luxury that belonged to people who had never had to claw their way through a day. I knew, in exhaustive detail, everything I was trying to get away from. I couldn't have told you a single thing I was moving toward, because I had never been allowed to want anything beyond making it to tomorrow.

So the turn didn't arrive as a triumphant moment of clarity. It arrived as a kind of vertigo. There was grief in it, grief for all the years I had spent only surviving, and grief for the simple fact that I was learning to want things at an age when most people have been doing it their whole lives. There were false starts, reaching for a version of myself that turned out to be someone else's idea of who I should be, then having to put it down. And there was the constant pull backward, because surviving was the thing I knew how to do, and becoming wasn't. More than once I reached toward something and then collapsed straight back into the old familiar crouch, certain I had been foolish to think I was allowed more than survival.

That collapse isn't failure. It's what learning to reach looks like after a lifetime of learning to flee. The reaching and the falling back are both part of the turn. You don't pivot from away to toward in a single clean motion. You do it the way you would turn a ship that has been pointed one direction for thirty years, slowly, with the old heading reasserting itself every time your attention drifts, until one day you notice you have actually been traveling the new way for a while.

What finally pointed me forward

What eventually gave the reach a direction was a decision, and I can tell you exactly where it started. Not long after I came forward about the abuse, with my mind quiet for the first time in memory, I noticed how much of my time I still spent sitting and turning over things that could never be changed. And a sentence kept surfacing, over and over, until I couldn't ignore it. I don't want to be that person anymore. If that was going to be true, I couldn't let my mind sit so still. I had to go and claim the things my life had been missing.

So I signed up for my GED. I had walked out of school in the ninth grade and had never once given myself credit for being intelligent, so I expected to fail. I took the pre-test and passed it. They entered me for the real thing, and I passed that too. It was a small achievement measured against a whole life, but it was a validating one, the first piece of evidence in a long time that the old verdict about not being good enough might simply be wrong. So I kept going. I took every program I could find that had anything to teach me about my situation or about getting ready for whatever came next. Then I heard the prison was offering college courses, signed up, and in time earned my associate's degree behind those walls.

But the thing that actually pointed me forward showed up alongside the education, not in it. The prison had a real need for peer suicide counselors, men on the inside who carried the title of Life Liner and sat with other men when they hit the bottom of their hope. That's where I first started helping people. Sitting with someone, understanding where he actually was, helping him turn his panic down a notch, was the first time in my life I felt something I can only call purpose.

One day I sat with a younger guy who had never been locked up before and had just come back from the medical ward after trying to end his life. I listened to his whole story, and in more places than I was ready for, it sounded like mine. It was the first time I ever handed pieces of my own story to someone standing where I had once stood. When I finished, he asked me two questions I've never forgotten. How do you do it. And how are you still alive. I told him the truth. I'm alive because I choose to be, because I've come to know there's something better and that it's on us to go and make it happen. I told him some of what I had already worked out in that cell, that the narratives running us on a loop aren't actually who we are, that they're only stories written into us, and that stories can be written over again. We talked a great deal in the short time he was there, and he got it. He understood what I was reaching for. I've thought many times since that I was teaching this framework out loud, to one frightened man, years before I had a single word to call it.

The turn didn't stop when I walked out of prison. It got tested in a way I never saw coming. I had gone in to sit with a doctor for the results of some tests, knowing something was off but bracing for nothing in particular, and what he said was a single word. Cancer. Then a two-minute silence while he read his charts, and when his voice came back I barely heard it. I caught the word treatments. I caught a promise that they would do everything they could. The rest was noise. I had never really known anyone with cancer except the few I had known who didn't survive it, and I drove home that day feeling like I had just been resentenced.

Sitting with that, I looked back across everything I had already lived through, and a different sentence rose up to meet the first. This can't be it. There's still so much I have to do. Sleep wouldn't come, and somewhere in that exhaustion, in the strange way a worn-down mind decides things before it knows it has decided, I found myself across a desk from a college representative, signing financial aid papers. Some part of me had concluded that if I enrolled in school, then this couldn't be the ending. I chose the courses on purpose, the ones that would deepen the work I already knew I was meant for, helping people climb out of addiction. Through the treatment that followed, I refused to let my mind live inside the illness. A purpose had presented itself, and I followed it instead. I became the student representative for my area, then vice president of the student association, and through that a non-voting member of the board of the foundation my school ran. The whole of that purpose, helping other people find their path, came to weigh more than everything the treatment was doing to me. And then, one day, the doctor told me it had worked. Remission. For the first time in a long while, I felt myself breathe.

Seven months later it came back, and this time they found a tumor in my lung. Surgery to remove part of the lung, and then the entire treatment again from the start. The second round was a harder thing altogether. It made me sicker, it kept me in the hospital longer, it took a real beating out of my body. But I didn't lose the thread. I did the opposite. I doubled down, found meaning in more of it, and finished building the purpose I had only sketched before. That's when I turned toward research. I took psychology courses and met, for the first time, several of the names I cite in this book. They weren't teaching me how to change. They were explaining, after the fact, the machinery behind changes I had already made by hand, finally handing me the why for parts of myself I had rebuilt without ever knowing the science. Outside of class I kept reading on my own, because I wanted to understand all of it. After a year, the doctor sat me down and said it again. Remission.

That's where the work turned from saving myself into something larger than me. I had no illusions about how I got to prison. I had caused real pain and real destruction, and I knew I carried a debt for it that I would never finish paying. But I also knew the only way a free man like me could begin to pay it. Not by drowning in what I had done, which helps no one, but by spending the rest of my life helping other people make a different choice than the one I made. By doing whatever I could to keep someone else off the road I had traveled, and to show them, with my own life as the proof, that it really can go another way. So I began telling my story in the open. I started mentoring without hiding any of it. I let people see the whole path that had led to the man now standing in front of them.

This is the phase where it would be easiest to start selling something, so I won't. None of it made the hard things stop being hard. The cancer was brutal. The grief was real. What the purpose did was give all of it a direction to be hard in. There's a vast difference between suffering that's only suffering and suffering that's the price of becoming someone, and the one thing that separates them is whether you're reaching toward something while you bear it. A why, it turns out, changes what you can endure on the way to it.

What meaning makes survivable

I lived my way into all of this with no framework and no vocabulary, first in a cell and then in the years after, by slowly turning from away to toward and discovering that a reason to live pulls harder than any fear pushes. Only later did I find the people who had mapped the same ground from the outside.

Viktor Frankl found it in a place far worse than mine. A psychiatrist who survived the concentration camps, he came out of that horror insisting that the people who endured the unendurable were so often the ones who had something to live for, some meaning out ahead of them that gave the suffering a shape. His line for it is the one I wish I had heard decades earlier: that a person who has a why to live can bear almost any how. That's precisely what the turn toward had given me. Not an easier road, but a reason that made the road bearable. He built a whole understanding of the human being around the idea that we're pulled forward by meaning, not just pushed around by our wounds, and that the search for that meaning is the most human thing we do.

Abraham Maslow mapped the same pull from another direction. His work describes how a human being, once no longer consumed by sheer survival and the scramble to meet basic needs, doesn't simply stop and rest. We turn, almost on our own, toward growth, toward becoming what we're capable of becoming. He gave that reaching a name, self-actualization, and he insisted it wasn't a luxury but a genuine human drive, as real as hunger. What he described as a natural turn toward growth was the exact thing I felt stir in that cell once the danger had finally quieted, the pull to stop merely existing and start becoming.

I didn't get this from Frankl or Maslow. I found my way here with no map, pushed by a hunger I couldn't have named at the time. Frankl and Maslow only put rigorous language to a discovery I had lived first: that a human being isn't only something to be repaired, but something that reaches.

Choosing the direction, not yet the destination

It's worth being clear about what this phase does and doesn't do, because it's easy to expect too much of it and then feel you've failed.

Transcend doesn't hand you a finished new self. It doesn't require you to have your whole future mapped, your purpose fully formed, your becoming worked out in detail. All it asks is that you turn. That you stop facing only what you're escaping and let yourself face, however unsteadily, what you might move toward. It's the choosing of a direction, not the arriving at a destination. The reach itself is the achievement here, not the grasp.

And that's exactly why there's another phase after this one. A direction isn't yet a life. Reaching toward who you want to become isn't the same as actually becoming it, and wanting a new identity, however sincerely, doesn't install it. The turn has to be made real, built into something you actually live rather than something you merely aim at, through what you repeatedly do. You've faced forward now. The next phase is where you start to walk.

Choosing the direction, not yet the destination

Install

You Become It by Doing It

✦

For a long time after I knew who I wanted to become, I had no idea how to actually become him. I had made the turn. I had a direction. What I didn't have was the man himself, and no amount of wanting him into existence made him show up.

What finally built him was almost embarrassingly unglamorous. I showed up. There was a recovery center I started going to, and at first I had no role there and no reason to be trusted, so I just came, every day, all day, and made myself useful in whatever small ways I could find. I did the things the person I wanted to be would do, over and over, long before I believed I was that person. I kept showing up when I felt like a fraud for showing up. And somewhere inside all that repetition, with no single moment I could point to afterward, I looked up one day and realized I had quietly become him. Not because I had declared it. Because I had done it, enough times, that it was simply true.

That's this phase. Install is where the self you chose in the last phase stops being an aspiration and becomes an actual identity, and it happens through one mechanism above all others: repeated action. You don't think your way into a new self, and you don't feel your way into one. You act your way into one, by doing what that person would do until the doing has built the person.

Not declared, done

This is exactly the place people get sold a lie, and I refuse to be the one selling it.

You don't install a new identity by announcing it. You don't become someone new by standing in the mirror and telling yourself you're confident, or worthy, or healed. We already threw that out, back when we talked about why you can't paint a new belief over an old one and expect it to hold. The affirmation is words, and words are cheap, and some honest part of you knows it the whole time you're reciting them. A self built out of declarations is a costume, and a costume comes off the moment anything real touches it.

What installs is evidence. Action is evidence. Every single time you do the thing the new person would do, you hand yourself a piece of proof that you're becoming that person, and the proof is undeniable in a way a sentence never is. You can't argue with what you have actually done. Say you're disciplined and some part of you scoffs. Get up early and do the hard thing forty mornings in a row and the scoffing has nothing left to stand on. The identity doesn't change because you insisted on it. It changes because you accumulated so much evidence of the new self that the old story could no longer be the truest account of who you are.

This is why the new identity has to be built, not claimed. And it's why it takes a while, and a lot of unremarkable repetition, and why there's no shortcut through this part that actually works.

The first self I built

Before the recovery center, before the jobs, before any of the rest of it, the very first self I ever installed was a sober one. It's still the clearest proof I have of how this phase actually works.

People assume that being locked up forces a person sober, that the walls do the work. That's simply not true. If a man inside wants to get drunk or high, he can find a way, and plenty do. The substances are there. So staying sober in that place was never the absence of a choice forced on me by my surroundings. It was a choice, made once and then made again every day after.

The choice didn't start gently. When I first came off alcohol my body was so dependent that I had to be hospitalized to survive the withdrawal. I hallucinated. Some of my organs began to shut down. It was as bad as anything I have lived through. But one thing here matters to how this phase works. That hospital stay isn't what made me quit. Fear of the physical damage isn't what made me quit. What made me quit was quieter than fear, and far more durable. I took an honest, sober look at my life and at the man I had become, and I didn't like him. So I decided, as a clear and conscious act, that I was done with all of it for good.

A decision like that isn't self-executing, though. Saying it once changed nothing on its own. What changed me was doing it, over and over, in a place practically built to test it. When the urge came, and early on it came hard, I would put myself in front of the plain fact of where I was and how I had gotten there, and in those first months the weight of that outweighed the wanting. I stayed away from the people who could put a drink or a pill in my hand. I made the sober choice again on the days I didn't feel like a sober man at all, which was most of them at the start. None of it was dramatic. It was the same small refusal, repeated, while I waited to become the kind of person for whom it would no longer be a refusal at all.

It took about a year of that before the urges stopped coming. And the day I learned the new self was truly built, I wasn't even trying to test it. A man approached me with a bottle he had found hidden away and asked if I wanted to buy it. Months earlier, just thinking about a drink could bring on a physical craving, almost the shakes. This time there was nothing. The offer landed in front of me and produced no pull, no quickening, no reaction at all. I turned it down without effort and went on with my day. The meaning of it only reached me that evening, when I was alone again and noticed the thing that was missing, the total quiet where the wanting used to live. My body hadn't so much as flinched. That was how I knew that drink and drugs no longer had any place in me, not because I was holding them off, but because the man I had built had no room left for them.

That's this entire phase in a single story. I didn't talk myself sober, and I didn't wait until I felt like a sober man to start behaving like one. I behaved like one first, by choice, one declined urge at a time, through a year of not yet believing it, until the behaving had quietly built a man for whom a bottle held out across a table was simply a non-event. The feeling came last. It always does.

Why it sits here

You can only install on cleared and chosen ground, which is the whole reason this phase comes sixth and not first.

If you try to build a new self on top of an old one you never dismantled, you get the affirmation trap all over again, a bright new identity laid over a foundation that still belongs to the old one, and the old one wins every time the pressure rises. That's why Nullify had to come first, to strip the authority from what was there. And you can't install a self you haven't yet chosen, which is why Transcend had to come before this, to point you somewhere worth building toward. Only now, with the old released and the direction set, is there solid ground to build on and a blueprint to build from. This is the phase where the actual construction happens.

The part nobody makes look good

I want to be honest about what this stretch actually feels like, because the gap between how it feels and how it looks from outside is wide, and that gap is where most people quit.

From the outside, installing a new identity looks like progress. From the inside, for a long time, it mostly feels like pretending. You're doing the things the new person does while still carrying the old person's beliefs underneath, which means you spend a good while acting as someone you don't yet believe you are. That isn't lying. That's the only way it has ever worked for anyone. But it produces a very specific discomfort, the sense of being an impostor in your own new life, waiting to be found out, certain that the competent or sober or steady version of you that other people are starting to see is a performance that will collapse any minute. I lived in that gap for a long time. I was building a real life and I was convinced, underneath, that I hadn't earned it and would be exposed.

And here's something nobody warned me about: that gap doesn't close once and stay closed. It came back at every new level I climbed to. The first time I was handed real responsibility, the old certainty that I would be found out returned as if I had never quieted it at all. Then came a job, and a harder one after that, and other opportunities I never imagined I would be trusted with, each one arriving with its own fresh wave of the same conviction, that I had wandered into a room I didn't belong in and that someone was about to notice. Every single time, the answer was the one I had learned at the recovery center. Show up. Act as the person the new role required before I believed I was him. Let the reps do their slow, unglamorous work until the level that felt borrowed started to feel like mine.

And it isn't a straight climb. There were days I didn't show up. There were stretches where I slid back into the old self's moves and the new identity felt like something I had made up. The reps don't announce themselves as working. You do them and you do them and nothing seems to shift, and then you look back over months and realize the person doing them now isn't the person who started. The discouragement in the middle isn't evidence that it isn't working. It's just what the middle feels like, because the evidence accumulates far slower than you want it to, and quietly, and mostly out of sight, until there's suddenly enough of it to stand on.

What carries you through that gap is simple to say and hard to do: you keep doing the reps while you wait for the belief to catch up to the behavior. Because it does catch up. The belief always lags the action, and the people who make it are the ones who keep acting through the lag instead of waiting to feel like the new person before they'll behave like them. You behave like them first. The feeling comes last.

What changed, eventually, wasn't that the feeling stopped arriving. It was that I stopped being ruled by it. Somewhere across all those rounds of installing myself into one more thing I was sure I couldn't do, the evidence stacked high enough to answer a deeper question than any single role could pose. Not *can I pull this off,* but *who am I.* And at some point I realized I actually knew, and that the knowing no longer rose and fell with whether one particular job was going well, because it was no longer propped on any single role at all. It rested on the long, accumulated proof of a person who had become, by doing, someone he could finally trust himself to be. That's what all the repetition is quietly building toward, underneath the tasks and the titles. Not competence at any one of them. A settled answer to the question of who you are.

How a habit becomes a self

I built my new self this way in real life, by showing up and repeating the actions of the person I wanted to be until I was him, long before I came across a single idea about how it worked. Later I found the people who had studied that exact process from the outside.

James Clear has described, about as plainly as anyone, how identity is actually built: through what you repeatedly do. His way of putting it is that every action you take is a vote for the type of person you're becoming, and that you build a new identity the way you would build anything, one small piece of evidence at a time, until the weight of evidence tips. That's precisely what those days at the recovery center were, votes, cast one after another for a person I wasn't sure I was yet, until the count itself made me into him. He came to it studying habits. I came to it living one rep at a time inside a life I was trying to rebuild. We met on the same conclusion: you become what you repeatedly do.

Carol Dweck mapped the ground underneath that. Her work shows that the self isn't a fixed thing you're stuck with but something that grows and changes through effort and process, and that the people who actually change are the ones who put their faith in the doing rather than in some fixed verdict about what they are or aren't capable of. That's the engine of this whole phase. Install only makes sense if a person can genuinely be rebuilt through practice, and her research is a large part of why we can say, with honesty rather than hope, that they can. What I had proved with my own repetition, she had demonstrated could be true for anyone willing to do the work.

I didn't get this from Clear or Dweck. I got here first through repetition, one unremarkable action laid on the last, and no theory to guide it. Clear and Dweck describe in their studies the very thing those reps had made real on the inside.

Built, but not yet proven

By the end of this phase you have something you didn't have before. Not a perfect new self, and not a finished one, but a real one, built out of actual evidence, standing on cleared ground, pointed in a direction you chose. You've done the things the new person does often enough that you are, in the ordinary practical sense, becoming them.

But there's a difference between a self that has been built and a self that has been tested, and you don't yet know which one you have. Everything installed so far has mostly been built under conditions you could manage, in the relative calm of deliberate practice. What you haven't faced yet is the hard day, the real provocation, the moment the old life reaches up and pulls and the new identity has to hold under genuine weight. A self isn't proven by how it performs when things are steady. It's proven by what it does under pressure. That's the next phase, and it's the one that tells you whether what you've installed is actually yours.

Test

What Only Pressure Reveals

✦

By the time I stepped into the leadership role, I had the confidence. The kind built the slow way in the last phase, out of years of showing up and doing the thing until the doing had made me into the person who could. I knew I could do the work. For the most part, I was right.

The old impostor feeling still showed up that first year, quieter now but present, the familiar whisper that I had talked my way into a room I didn't belong in. I showed up anyway, the way I had learned to. And the work answered the whisper better than any argument could. I was good at it. For two years I excelled. I took on more than the job asked for. I sat on committees. I was put through an emerging leaders program. Most of all, I built a peer team from the ground up, a real one, diverse and capable, and I led it well. That's not me being generous with myself. It's simply what happened, and it matters that I say it plainly, because of what came later.

Because this is the phase where the self you've built meets the world on the world's terms, and finds out what it's actually made of. Install builds the new identity under conditions you can mostly manage, in roles you walk toward on purpose. Test is what happens when the pressure isn't chosen. When life reaches up without warning and leans on the thing you built, hard, to see whether it holds. And the first honest thing I have to tell you about my own test is that it didn't.

The year it broke

In my third year, several people in my family got sick. Not briefly, and not in ways that resolved. The weight of it built and built until it was the largest thing in my life, and somewhere in carrying it I stopped showing up fully for the job. I backslid. The work I had excelled at for two years started to slip, and now I was being spoken to about it, and not kindly. The impostor feeling, which had gone quiet, came back at full strength, and it found me already worn down. My own mental health started to give under the combined weight of their illness and the old story rising back up, until I had to take a leave of absence just to get my head clear.

When I came back, it felt different. The interest was gone. The excitement that had carried me was gone. And then I got written up. To my old self, that write-up wasn't a piece of feedback. It was a verdict. It was proof of the thing I had always secretly feared, that I didn't belong, that the whole competent version of me had been a performance, and that I had finally been found out. Not long after, I no longer worked there.

If I had stopped the story there, the old self would have won, because the old self had an explanation ready and it was a lie. The lie was: you were always an impostor, and now everyone knows. But that explanation couldn't survive a single honest look at the evidence. Two years of real mastery don't belong to an impostor. The team I built was real. The work I did was real. Whatever had gone wrong in that last year, "I never belonged here" wasn't it. The verdict didn't fit the facts.

What the hell happened

So once I was out of it, out of the job and out of the daily weight of it, I asked myself the only question that mattered. What the hell happened. Understand, this wasn't a framework yet. I had no eight phases to consult, no map to retrace. I had only my own life and a question I couldn't put down. How had I made so much change everywhere else, change that held, and why had it worked everywhere but here. I went back over every step. I held the two good years up against the collapse and refused to let the collapse be the whole story until I understood it.

And then it landed, the connection that unlocked the rest. That pushback reminded me of prison.

For most of that last year, every time I went to my supervisor with what my team needed, I got pushback. The need got denied, or the budget got blamed, or I was told it didn't make sense. Most of our supervisions were clinical, not peer supervision at all, which makes sense in hindsight: my supervisor was a clinician with no real experience working with peers, let alone overseeing a whole team of them. Pushing the team forward became a constant struggle against that wall. And the longer I stood at that wall, the more the whole thing started to feel institutional. Like the dignity of my team was being stripped. Like peer work was an afterthought, which in a lot of respects, inside that system, it was.

I know that place. I had felt exactly that before, in the one institution built to strip dignity on purpose. The moment I saw the resemblance, something I had buried for years came up into the light. I had given that supervisor the weight of an institution, and I had gone into the same posture I had learned behind the walls. Defense. Brace. Survive it. And that posture had blinded me to the obvious thing a free man would have done. I could have gone over my supervisor's head. I could have taken the case to the people who were actually invested in the peer role and laid it out plainly, the team's needs and the constant denial of them. That door was there the whole time. I never even saw it, because the old wiring told me that you don't challenge the institution, you only endure it.

What the test had found

Here's what the test had actually found. Years earlier, in prison, I had built a new self in the one place designed to make that impossible, and I had given myself back a dignity that place was built to take. I had done deep work. But there was one belief I had never gone back and dismantled, because I had never needed to. The belief that institutional authority is absolute, that in front of it you're powerless, that the only move is to protect yourself and wait it out. I built an entire new identity standing on top of that belief without ever questioning it, and it stayed quiet for years, because no room I walked into ever recreated the feeling. Until one did. And the moment it did, the old wiring fired exactly as it had been built to, and it took down two years of good work with it.

What I did next, I did on pure instinct, with no idea it was anything so formal as a method. I started stripping the narrative. I asked the question that does the actual work: that place is gone, it has no authority in my life anymore, so why am I handing my supervisor the same weight it used to have. Why am I letting that pushback put me into a survival posture I built in a cell. The moment I could see the belief instead of looking out through it, its grip started to loosen. I could finally separate the two things I had fused: an under-prepared supervisor inside a system that genuinely undervalued the work, and the institution in my head that I had never stripped of its power. They weren't the same. I had been fighting the second one while thinking I was dealing with the first.

I want to be straight about my part, because understanding what happened isn't the same as excusing it. The illness in my family was real and the wall I kept hitting was real, but the choice to go silent and stop showing up was mine, and it came from a belief I had carried for years and never examined. I'm not apologizing for being human under that much weight. But I own what I did with it. I let an old story stop me cold instead of doing the thing the new self was fully capable of doing.

Why it could only be hindsight

Here's the part I most want you to take from this. I didn't see any of it in the moment. I saw it all afterward, in hindsight, and hindsight is always perfect. For a long time I beat myself up about that, about how obvious it looked once I was out of it. But I have come to understand why it could only be hindsight, and that understanding is the whole reason this phase exists.

You can't see something clearly while its authority over you is still intact and you're still sitting inside its scope. Until you understand the full scope of a thing, and redefine what it means in your life, and strip it of the power your mind handed it, you won't see it clearly. It will only be revealed in hindsight. Some beliefs will never show themselves to quiet reflection, no matter how honest you are, because they only wake up when real pressure recreates the conditions that formed them. That's exactly what a test is for. It isn't there to grade you. It's there to surface the one thing reflection could never reach.

Mastery, and the grit to return

I lived all of this with none of the research yet in front of me. Later I found the people who had mapped it from the outside.

Albert Bandura spent his career on a single idea that sits underneath this whole chapter: that durable belief in yourself isn't built by being told you're capable, but by mastery, by actually getting through hard things and accumulating the proof. That's why "impostor" was never the true account of me. I had two years of genuine mastery on the record, and you can't reason an impostor into that. But his work also names exactly where I broke. The test found the one domain where I had never had a mastery experience at all: standing my ground, as a free man, against institutional authority. Everywhere else I had the proof. There, I had only the old prison wiring, untested and intact. The framework had reached every part of me except the part that place had built, because nothing had pressed on it until then.

Angela Duckworth gave language to the other half. Her work on grit describes the people who hold on through setbacks and keep going, and I want to be honest about how that did and didn't look in me. In the moment, I didn't show grit. I went on the defensive and I stopped showing up. My grit, such as it was, came later, and it came as the return. It was the refusal to accept the impostor verdict and walk away believing it. It was going back, out of the wreckage, to find out what had actually happened and to finish the piece of work I had missed. Grit wasn't me never falling. It was me not staying down once I understood what had knocked me over.

I didn't get any of this from Bandura or Duckworth. I learned all of this the expensive way, in the loss of a job I had been good at. Bandura and Duckworth only put evidence behind what that failure had driven into me.

The proof it held

That's the diagnosis. What I haven't told you yet is whether the repair actually took, because a repair you never see tested is only a theory. So here's the proof. Since that job I have stood in front of institutional authority in its strongest form and felt nothing of the old collapse.

Some time after I left, I interviewed at a prison mental hospital in a neighboring state. I want you to notice the setting, because my mind certainly did. A prison. The exact kind of institution that had built the old wiring in the first place. The interview ran two hours, with a tour worked into it, and across all of it they questioned my leadership, my background, and my time inside. The questions were hard. More than once it felt less like an interview than an interrogation.

That's exactly the room that would once have shut me down. Authority, scrutiny, my whole record held up to the light, an institution leaning its weight on me and asking me to justify myself. It was the old wiring's home ground. And it didn't shut me down. I answered every question with authority and with expertise. I didn't brace, I didn't shrink, and I didn't drop into the survival posture I had built in a cell and carried for years. I sat in that room as a free man who knew his work and knew his worth. And it went the opposite way from the job that broke. The director told me, right there in the interview, that he had learned a great deal from me, and that the vision I brought for what a peer team could be went well beyond his own. I was offered the position before the interview was even finished.

That's what a passed test looks like. The same pressure, the same kind of room, the very conditions that had taken down the role before, and this time the self held. Not because I gritted my teeth harder. Because the ground underneath had changed. The belief that institutional authority is absolute, that in front of it you can only brace and endure, had been pulled out from under me on purpose, back in the repair. And with that belief gone, there was nothing left in that room for the old wiring to grab.

Your dormant one

Mine was institutional authority, learned in the most extreme version of that lesson a person can get. That's what makes it useful here, not because your version will be as severe, but because the severity made the mechanism impossible to miss. Yours might be a parent whose approval still runs you in rooms they'll never enter. A church, a school, a first boss, some early system that taught you something about power, or worth, or your place, that you've never gone back and questioned, because life hasn't yet put you in the room that wakes it up. You can build a strong new self and still be carrying one of these, dormant, load-bearing, waiting. You won't find it by thinking hard. You'll find it the day something leans on it and it gives, and then you get to do what I did, and trace the give back to its source.

This is also the phase most likely to knock the wind out of you, because a real test can break something before it teaches you anything. If you put your new self under pressure and it buckles, that can be a hard place to stand, and it's wise to have someone in reach if it happens, a coach, a therapist, a trusted person. Not because you can't do this work. Because the work is real and so is the weight. The going-back is yours to do. The support is just there in case the test hits harder than you expected.

Built, then proven

A failed test isn't the end of the framework. It's the framework working. The self that broke in that job wasn't weak. It was unfinished, and the test did the one thing nothing else could. It told me precisely where. I went back to the earliest work and dismantled the belief I had stood on without knowing it was there, and the self that came through that was more whole than the one that walked in, because now it was built on ground I had actually checked.

Which leaves one phase. Having built a self, and tested it, and gone back to repair what the test exposed, there's a last move. Learning to live from it without holding on so tightly. To stop bracing and proving and simply let it be who you are. That's where we end.

Yield

When You Stop Holding It Up

✦

There came a point, and I couldn't tell you the date, when I noticed I had stopped trying to be the man I had become. I was just being him. The choosing had gone quiet. The bracing had gone quiet. The work of holding myself in the new shape, which had taken everything I had for years, had somehow become the shape itself. I wasn't performing it anymore. I wasn't defending it. I was simply living as it.

That's the last phase, and it's the strangest one to write about, because it's the one that arrives by letting go rather than by effort. Every phase before this asked you to do something. Yield asks you to stop doing one particular thing. To stop holding the new self up by force, and let it stand on its own. To stop proving it, and simply be it.

The word matters, because it pulls in two directions at once, and the phase needs both. To yield is to stop forcing, to release your grip, to quit straining against the current and let it carry you. And to yield is also what a field does at harvest, when all the planting and the tending finally come back as something you can live on. This phase is both. It's the release of the effort, and it's the harvest of everything the effort built.

The day it showed itself

The settling itself came so gradually that I couldn't name the day it happened. But there was one day it showed itself to me plainly, and it was anything but quiet.

By then my life had gone quietly normal. I had stopped worrying about what people thought of me, because I knew my own worth, and my Monday felt the same as my Friday. Steady. Unremarkable. Then, one weekend, I pulled into a parking spot at a store, got out of my truck, and a man came at me, yelling obscenities and making threats.

I need you to understand what the old me would have done with that, because the contrast is the whole point. The old me, the one carrying the imprint that you strike before you're struck, wouldn't have waited to find out whether the threat was real. I would have hit him first. That was the rule I had lived by for years, and it was part of what had landed me in prison.

That's not what happened. He was furious because he believed I had taken a spot he was waiting for, though there had been no one there when I pulled in. So I pointed, calmly, to my dash cam, and I told him, look, if I cut you off, I apologize, let me check the camera, and if I did, the spot is yours, no big deal. He kept arguing. I let him finish. Then I told him, I'm sorry you're having a bad day, but I'm not the one who ruined it, and I'm not your target here. And I said I was walking away. And I did.

There were no shakes afterward. No replay, no adrenaline crash, no second-guessing. I got my groceries. Because the man who handled that wasn't managing an urge to hit him. The urge wasn't there to manage. The self that would have swung hadn't been suppressed. It had been replaced. That's what I mean by yielding. The new man didn't have to win that encounter, or prove a thing in it, or even work at staying calm. He just was calm, because calm was finally who he was.

Why it comes last

You can only yield what you have actually built and tested. That's why this comes at the end and nowhere else. You can't relax into a self that isn't there yet, and you can't rest in one that has never held under weight. If you try to yield too early, before the building and before the proving, you don't get peace. You get complacency, or denial, a person insisting they have arrived because they are tired of the work. Real yielding is earned. It's the rest that comes after the self has been built by your own hands, and proven under real pressure, and repaired where it broke. Only then is there something solid enough to lay your weight down on.

I want to be careful here, because this is the place a lesser book would lie to you and tell you that you arrive, the struggle ends, and you're fixed. That's not what happens, and it's not what I'm promising. The old self still speaks. There are still mornings the old voice shows up with its old verdict, that I'm not enough, that I don't belong, that I'm still the sum of the worst things about me. Yielding didn't delete that voice. What changed is that I no longer hand it the keys. It can speak. It doesn't get to drive. That's the difference between a self you're forever defending and a self you've settled into. You stop needing the old voice to be silent. You just stop giving it authority it no longer earns.

The thing I had to set down

The biggest thing I had to yield was the need to prove I had changed. For years, underneath everything, I was building a case. To the people who knew what I had done. To the institutions that had filed me under my worst day. To myself, who was the hardest of all to convince. Every good thing I did carried a second, quieter job: see, I'm not who you think. And there's a point where carrying that case becomes its own prison. Yielding was setting it down. It was the day I realized I no longer needed anyone's verdict, including my own, to be who I am. I had become him. The proof was the life, and the life was already there. I could stop arguing for it and just live it.

Part of that meant making peace with the entire story, including the heaviest part of it, because it would be cheap to talk about integration and leave that out. There's a night I can never take back. A life was lost because of what I did and what I failed to do. I have never looked for a way to make that smaller than it is, and I never will. Understanding how a person ends up there isn't the same as excusing it, and I hold both of those at once. What yielding gave me wasn't relief from that. It was the ability to carry it as part of who I am without it being the whole of who I am. To hold the full weight of what I did, and the full dignity of who I have become, in the same two hands, and not drop either one. A settled self isn't one that has erased its history. It's one that can hold all of it and still stand.

I have been handed things since that, earlier in my life, would have undone me. Twice I've faced cancer. There was a version of me, not so long ago, that would have met that news by scrambling, or raging, or reaching for something to numb it, or collapsing into the old certainty that I was being punished for what I was. That's not who met it. What met it was someone who already knew who he was, and didn't need a crisis to tell him. I'm not saying I met it without fear. I'm saying the fear didn't get to redefine me. The self held. That's what a yielded self does. It doesn't promise you an easy road. It promises that the road won't turn you back into who you used to be.

The people from the beginning

Making peace with my own story eventually meant making peace, where it was possible, with the people who had marked it at the start. I want to tell you how some of that landed, because yielding isn't only something that happens inside you. Sometimes it shows up in the relationships the old wounds had wrecked.

My father, whose leaving wrote the very first line of who I thought I was, came back into my life while I was still in prison. We talked. We reconciled. Today we have a strong relationship, the kind the boy who once decided he was the reason people leave could never have pictured for himself. My brother and I are in regular contact. He lives most of a country away, so we don't see each other often, but the line between us is open and steady. And some of the friends from my using days are still in my life, except everything about that is different now. None of us drink or use anymore, so when we get together at this age we aren't chasing anything. We sit with each other through the real challenges of grown lives, and we're each other's sounding board. The same circle that once helped me disappear now helps me stay.

I'm not going to tell you every thread tied off neatly, because that wouldn't be honest, and not everyone in a story like mine is someone you reconcile with. But the imprints that began with people leaving didn't get the final say over how those relationships had to end. Some of them came back around. That, too, is part of what the work gives back.

When the good stops being for anything

Somewhere in all of this, the work of helping other people stopped being evidence and started being identity. For a long time, every person I helped was, somewhere underneath, a brick in the case for my own redemption. Now it's just what I do, because it's who I am, the way water runs downhill. I don't help people to prove I'm good. I help people because a person like the one I became helps people. The motive quieted, and the thing itself remained. That's one of the surest signs I know that a new identity has actually settled. The good you do stops being for anything. It's just yours.

Why this book exists

There's one more piece of evidence that I have yielded, and you're holding it.

For most of my life I never wanted to be seen at all. After prison, I wanted my life kept private, and by then it wasn't fear that wanted it. I simply didn't feel any need to stand in a spotlight. I had nothing to prove and no wish to perform, and for a long time that was enough.

What changed was the purpose. The one I had built, helping people find their own path to a better life, whatever that path needs to look like for them, came to outweigh the privacy. Too many people had asked me the same questions. How did you build a life. How did you hold the positions you have held. How did you get through barriers that were put there precisely to keep people like you out. Hearing it over and over sent me back across my own road, and when I looked carefully I saw something I hadn't fully seen while I was walking it. There had been an actual map. There were real steps, in a real order, that had carried me from who I was to who I am. Once I could see the map, keeping it to myself felt wrong. So I made it public. I wrote it down. You're reading the result.

That decision is its own kind of yielding. The old me guarded his story to survive. This book is the opposite move. It's me holding the whole of who I became loosely enough to hand it to a stranger, because it might help. I'm not protecting it anymore. I'm giving it away. And that, in the end, is the legacy I want to leave behind, not the worst day of my life, and not even the climb out of it, but the map itself, in someone else's hands, carrying them somewhere better.

An identity that keeps growing

I settled into all of this by living it, with no vocabulary for it at the time. The language came later, from two people who studied exactly this kind of arrival.

Robert Kegan spent his career describing how adults actually grow, and the move he mapped is the move this whole phase is made of. Early on, he says, we're run by the things inside us. We can't see them, because we're looking out through them, and they have us. Growth, in his account, is the slow turning of those things from something that has you into something you have, something you can hold and look at and live with instead of being driven by. That's the exact difference between every earlier phase and this one. For years my new identity was something I was inside of, gripping, working to maintain. Yielding was the turn where it became something I simply hold, lightly enough that it can even keep growing, because a settled self isn't a frozen one. He gave the precise shape to what the release had felt like from the inside.

Patricia Deegan came to it from her own life, which is why it lands with the weight it does. Told as a young woman that her diagnosis meant a small and managed future, she refused that verdict and spent her life showing that recovery isn't the same as cure. It's not a finish line where you're declared fixed. It's a way of living a full and meaningful life as the person you are, limitations and all, on your own terms rather than the ones an institution assigned you. That's yielding, exactly. Not the erasure of everything you have carried, but the decision to live a real life from the self you reclaimed, and to stop waiting for anyone's permission to do it. She put words to what I had done without knowing its name. I had stopped living the future I was handed, and started living the one I had built.

I didn't learn this from Kegan or Deegan. I arrived here by living it, one quiet release at a time, with no name for any of it. Kegan and Deegan lend the shape and the proof to a settling my own life had completed years before.

Your own opening hand

Mine settled after about as much building and breaking as a life can hold, which is the only reason I can say what I'm about to say with any authority. If it can settle after that, it can settle after anything. Your building may have been quieter than mine. Your self may have been assembled out of ordinary disappointments rather than catastrophes. It doesn't matter. The yield is the same move for everyone. There comes a point where you have done the work, and the self you built is real, and the only thing left between you and peace is your own grip on it. Yielding is opening your hand. It's letting the self you made hold you for a change, instead of the other way around.

And that's the eighth phase. Imprint showed you what was stamped into you. Deconstruct took apart the beliefs it left behind. Expose brought the hidden things into the light. Nullify stripped the old patterns of their power. Transcend pointed you somewhere worth going. Install built the new self by hand. Test proved it under fire and sent you back to finish what was missed. And Yield is where you finally set down the effort and let what you built be who you are.

The framework ends here. But you don't, because a self that has settled still has the whole rest of a life in front of it. What that looks like day after day, and how this work sits alongside the professionals who walk the road with you, is where we turn next.

PART THREE

Carrying It Forward

A Complement Not a Replacement

Your Work, Your Way

✦

This work was built for two kinds of people, and both of them are doing it right.

The first kind does it inside a setting already built for this sort of thing. With a therapist. With a peer specialist or a recovery coach. In a group, a program, a treatment plan. The second kind does it on their own, at a kitchen table, with this book and a notebook and nobody watching. Before anything else in this chapter: neither one of those is the correct way to do this. The correct way is the one you choose. This is your work. It was always going to be your work. And the respect I owe you, from the first page to the last, is the respect of your own autonomy to decide how you walk it.

So when I call this a complement to professional care, here's what I mean. It builds on the work professionals do; it doesn't stand in for it. Drop this framework into a therapist's office, a peer's caseload, a recovery coach's practice, and it doesn't compete with what's already happening there. It hands them, and the person in front of them, a tool that gets real results, and it makes the role go further. That's what a complement is.

Both paths are real

I'll say plainly that I'm not anti-clinical, and I never will be. I wouldn't be alive to write this without clinical care. Clinicians kept me breathing through stretches when I couldn't have kept myself breathing, and medication steadied a mind that wasn't safe to be alone in. I owe the clinical world real debts, and nothing in this book is a reason for anyone to walk away from treatment that's keeping them well. If you're in care, stay in care, and bring this work into it.

And if you're not in care, and you have no plans to be, and you want to do every bit of this on your own, that's not the lesser version of the work. It's not the consolation path for people who couldn't get the real thing. It is the real thing.

None of that means this work does everything. It does one thing, the deep reconstruction of who you are, and it does it well. It's not a diagnosis. It's not medication. It's not crisis care, and it can't treat a condition that's medical rather than motivational. Those are real, and they're not this, and a person is allowed to need both. Knowing what this is and what it isn't is part of using it well.

Who I had beside me

I can tell you both paths are real because I have walked both, in one life.

For long stretches of my own rebuilding, I had a clinician on standby. I point to that on purpose, because it's the very thing I'm encouraging here, lived out in my own story. There was someone trained in my corner, available when the work turned up something that needed a trained eye, someone I could bring the heavy material to and not be alone with it. That mattered. I won't pretend it didn't, and I won't recommend to you a kind of support I didn't lean on myself.

But it wasn't like that the whole way through, and here's where I have to be honest about the shape of my own road. The hardest early rebuilding, the years inside, I did with no professional within reach, because there wasn't one to reach for. And the work I would only understand much later as the last two phases, the testing of who I had become and the settling into it, I also did entirely on my own. There was no clinician beside me for that part. By the time that work came, the framework wasn't even a framework yet. It was just me, retracing my own steps, trying to understand why the self I had built had buckled and how to make it whole again.

What I had then was my wife. When something came up that I needed to get out of my own head, I said it out loud to her. Not so she would fix it. Not even so she would advise me. Only so I could hear it plainly, spoken into the air between two people, and know that it was real. There's a particular kind of clarity that only comes when you say the true thing out loud to someone safe and hear how it actually sounds. A thought you have carried in silence changes the moment it becomes a sentence another person hears. That's what a sounding board is. Sometimes you don't need an answer from anyone. You need to hear your own truth said aloud, and witnessed, so it stops being a private fog and becomes something solid you can stand on and answer.

That's the whole range of it, in one life. A clinician on standby for part of the road. No one at all for the hardest early part. And for the work that finished it, my wife across the table, not steering, just listening, so I could hear myself clearly. Every one of those was real work, and all of it counted.

Someone you trust on standby

So here's the one thing I would gently encourage, no matter which path you're on, and it's not a requirement and it's not supervision. It's wise to have someone you trust on standby. Not someone to do the work for you, or to approve of it, or to grade it. Just someone who knows that you decided to do this, someone who can walk with you through whatever feelings the work stirs up, someone who can be a sounding board on the day you need to say a hard thing out loud and hear it land in another person.

That someone can be a clinician, the way one was for me through part of this road. It can just as easily be a wife, a friend, a sponsor, a sibling, anyone steady who has earned your trust, the way mine was for me through the rest. The point isn't their credential. The point is that you're not carrying the heaviest moments of this entirely by yourself, and that when something rises up that you didn't see coming, there's a hand already there, and a voice you can say the hard thing out loud to.

There's one exception to all of this autonomy, and I'll name it plainly because lives are the stakes. A crisis isn't the time for a framework. If you're in real danger, put the book down and reach for help, immediately, whatever help is closest. This work is for rebuilding over time. It was never meant to stand between a person in crisis and the care that moment needs.

More tools, more hands

I know where this work fits because fitting it there is my own job. I'm a peer. I sit alongside clinicians, doing the part the lived experience makes possible and the training doesn't. When I tell someone I have been where they are, it's not a technique. It's a fact, and it opens a door a credential alone often can't. I don't see the person in front of me as a case. I see someone whose life, however it looks from outside, makes complete sense from the inside, because mine did too. That stance doesn't replace the clinical one. It reaches a different part of the person, and together they reach more of them than either reaches alone.

That's the whole idea of this book in one sentence. More tools, in more hands, reaching more of the person. Never fewer.

So take what helps and leave what doesn't. Do this in an office or do it at your kitchen table. Do it with a team around you or do it with one trusted person a phone call away. Every one of those is a real and right way to do this work, because the work is yours and the choosing is yours.

With that settled, a question remains. Once the self is built, and tested, and finally yours, how do you actually live from it, day after ordinary day. That's where we turn next.

Living From the New Identity

What the Work Was For

✦

I want to tell you what living from the new identity actually looks like, and the first thing to know is how ordinary it is. There's no triumphant music. For all the drama it took to get here, the building and the breaking and the going back, the destination turns out to be a regular Tuesday.

For most of my life, an ordinary day started with a verdict. Before my feet hit the floor, the old story was already running, that I was broken, that I didn't belong, that I was the sum of the worst things about me, and the whole day got spent either proving it or outrunning it. Living from the new identity means I wake up and that voice isn't the first thing in the room. Most mornings it's not in the room at all. I just get up, and I'm myself, and the day is mine to live instead of survive. That's the reward. It's quieter than you would expect, and it's everything.

When the map becomes the territory

Somewhere along the way the eight phases stopped being steps I took and became the way I see. I don't sit down and run a process when something knocks me sideways now. It happens closer to instinct. Something stings, and almost before I've decided to, I'm already asking the old questions. What did I just make that mean. Is that interpretation true, or is it old wiring. Whose voice is that, really. The framework went from something I did to something I'm made of. That's what it means for this work to take. You don't carry the map forever. Eventually you become someone who simply knows the territory.

Life keeps coming

Living from the new identity doesn't mean life stops coming for you. It comes for everyone, settled or not. There will be losses you didn't choose and pressures you didn't invite, and some of them will press on exactly the places you thought were finished. I know this better than most, because the hardest test of my rebuilt self came years after I thought the rebuilding was done, and it sent me all the way back to the beginning to find a belief I had never dismantled.

That's not the exception to living from a new identity. That's part of it. The difference now is that when something cracks, I'm not lost. I know what cracked, and I know how to mend it, because I have the map and I've walked it before. A setback is no longer proof that I'm broken. It's just information about where the next piece of work is. You'll loop. Everyone loops. Living from the self means looping with a map instead of looping in the dark.

A self that keeps growing

And the self you live from isn't a finished monument you spend the rest of your life dusting. It keeps growing. The person I am now isn't the person I installed years ago, and he isn't supposed to be. A settled identity isn't a frozen one. It's solid enough to stand on and loose enough to keep becoming, and living from it means letting it go on changing instead of clutching the version of yourself that got you this far. You didn't do all this work to trade one rigid identity for another. You did it to become someone who can keep growing for the rest of your life.

It lives in your life, not your head

Here's the thing I most want you to understand about this. The new identity isn't a feeling you have about yourself. It's not a private sense of worth you check on in the mirror. It's a life. It lives in how you treat the people closest to you, in the work you actually do, in how you handle the day that falls apart. I don't know that I've changed because I feel good about myself. I know it because of how I show up now, for my wife, for the people I work with, for the stranger having the worst day of their life in front of me. The proof of a rebuilt self is never in your head. It's in your life, where other people can feel it.

And there's something that tends to happen once you're living from a self that's no longer fighting for its own survival. You have room for other people in a way you never did before. When you're not spending all your energy holding yourself together, that energy goes somewhere, and for a lot of people, myself included, it runs toward helping someone else do what you did. I'm not saying you owe the world that. I'm saying a self at peace tends to overflow, and the overflow usually runs toward others. Some of the best parts of my life came out of that overflow.

Peace isn't the absence of trouble

None of this adds up to a life without trouble. I've faced serious illness more than once since I settled into who I am. I've lost things, and grieved, and had hard years. Living from the new identity didn't buy me a smooth road. What it bought me was the ability to walk a rough one without losing myself on it. The peace I'm talking about isn't the absence of trouble. It's the presence of a self that holds when trouble comes. That's a different and far better thing, because trouble is the one guarantee, and a self that holds is something you get to keep no matter what arrives.

Your version of this will look nothing like mine, and it's not supposed to. You'll live from your new identity in your own ordinary days, in a life I will never see, in a shape that's yours to design. There's no correct picture of what a rebuilt life is supposed to look like. There's only the quiet, daily fact of living as yourself, on your own terms, in whatever form your life takes. That's the whole prize. Not a particular life. Your life, lived by you, as the person you rebuilt.

✦

This is what waits on the other side of the eight phases. Not a finish line, but a way of living. Ordinary, ongoing, yours. Which leaves only one thing left, and it's the thing this entire book has been walking toward. It isn't enough for me to tell you that this is possible. The rest was never mine to write. That's where we end, and where you come in.

The Invitation

Begin Where You Are

✦

This whole book has been my story and the shape of the thing I built out of it. This last part is about you.

I have told you, as plainly as I know how, that a person can be rebuilt. That who you are was constructed, and what was constructed can be reconstructed. That you're not stuck being whoever you were told to be. I didn't tell you any of that to impress you with my survival. I told you because it's true for you, and because somewhere in the reading of it, I'm hoping a part of you started to wonder if it might be.

So here, at the end, there's only one question left, and it's not mine to answer. It's yours. Not whether change is possible: we've settled that. It's whether you'll begin.

The voice that says not you

I know what's probably happening as you read this, because I know the voice. It's already talking. It's telling you that this was a good story but that you're different. That your situation is too far gone, or your past too heavy, or your wiring too old. That it worked for me and it won't work for you, that you're the exception, the one person this doesn't reach.

I want you to notice that voice, because that voice isn't the truth about you. It's the exact thing this entire book is built to take apart. It's the old verdict, doing the only job it knows how to do, which is to keep you where you are. It was wrong about me in every way a thing can be wrong. It's wrong about you too.

I'm not inviting you to this from a mountaintop. I'm inviting you from the bottom of the same kind of hole you may be sitting in right now. I built a self in a cell, out of the wreckage of just about every way a life can go wrong. I'm not saying that to wave my story around again. I'm saying it because it's the only credential that matters here. If a person can be rebuilt from there, a person can be rebuilt from wherever you are. Your road may be quieter than mine was. That doesn't make you less able to walk it. The thing that has to change is the same for all of us. It isn't the size of what happened to you. It's the meaning you made of it, and meaning can always be remade.

An open door, not a push

This is an invitation, not an instruction. I mean that. You don't have to do any of this. No one can make you, and I wouldn't respect you by trying. The whole of this work, from the first phase to the last, only ever belongs to the person who chooses it freely. So I'm not going to push you through the door. I'm going to do the one thing this book was written to do, which is hold it open, and tell you, with everything I have, that what's on the other side is real, that it can be yours, and that the choosing is entirely your own.

If you do decide to begin, hear this clearly. You don't have to do it all at once. You don't have to fix your whole life today. You don't even have to believe it will work. You only have to begin, with one honest look at one thing you have always taken as simply true about yourself. That's the whole of the first step. Not a leap. A look. You begin where you are, as you are, with what you have, on the day you decide to. There's no readiness to wait for. The readiness is the deciding.

This book was the why of it. The why had to come first, because no one does hard work they don't understand the reason for. The how is waiting for you whenever you turn toward it, the actual work of the eight phases, ready to be walked one at a time. But that's the next thing. The first thing is simply the turn toward it.

The only thing that can stop you

I'll tell you one last hard truth, and I'll tell it kindly, because it's the most hopeful thing in this book. There's only one thing in the entire world that can keep this from you. It isn't your past. It isn't your diagnosis, or your record, or how far down you've gone, or how long you've been down there. Every one of those is workable. I have watched every one of them be worked. The only thing that can truly stop you is deciding never to start. And that, like everything else in this book, is yours. Which means the door is never actually locked. It only waits.

So I'll leave you the way I've wanted to from the first page. You're not the worst thing that happened to you. You're not the worst thing you've done. You're not the verdict that got handed to you before you were old enough to refuse it. Those are old conclusions, and conclusions can be unmade. Who you actually are is still yours to build, and it has been the whole time.

The door is open. I'm holding it. Begin where you are.

Acknowledgments

I didn't rebuild my life alone, and I didn't write this book alone either. Everything in these pages was made possible by people who refused to give up on me, often long before I had given them any good reason to keep trying.

To my wife, Jessica: you have seen me at my worst and stayed anyway, and a great deal of who I am now is owed to that. Thank you for being the proof, every day, of the kind of support this book argues no one should have to do without.

To my family, and to the friends who became family: thank you for holding open a door I once thought I had closed for good.

To the professionals who treated me, counseled me, and believed recovery was possible for me when I couldn't believe it myself: this book makes the case that what you do matters, and it makes that case because of you.

To the peers and the recovery community who showed me that lived experience isn't something to hide but something to offer: you handed me the work that became my life.

And to the people I have walked beside as a peer specialist and recovery coach, who trusted me with their stories: you tested every idea in this book in the only place that counts, which is a real life. I am grateful beyond what I know how to say.

Thank you, finally, to you for reading. I hope it returns to you many times over.

Acknowledgments

About the Author

Alfred Brissette Jr. is a Certified Peer Specialist and Certified Recovery Coach, and the creator of the IdentiNova framework. He holds a bachelor's degree in organizational and community development. He developed IdentiNova out of his own life long before he found it confirmed in research: a life marked by early abandonment and abuse, addiction, incarceration, serious illness, and homelessness, and one that came out the other side rebuilt rather than broken.

After years of doing this work one conversation at a time, he set out to put what he had learned into a form other people could use. The result is a two-part body of work: the IdentiNova workbook, which walks a person through the eight phases step by step, and this companion, which tells the story of where the framework came from and why it holds. He has also published several articles on the importance of peer work and on why change is possible.

His work reaches well beyond the page. He advocates at the State House level for prison reform and for housing policy reform for people returning from incarceration, and he received a State Citation from the State of Rhode Island for his work as a recovery coach.

Today he works as a peer specialist and recovery coach in Massachusetts, drawing on lived experience to help others understand what shaped them and rebuild who they choose to be. He is currently developing a facilitator training to put IdentiNova into the hands of the people who do this work professionally.

He can be reached at IdentiNova.com or IdentiNovaBooks@proton.me.

About the Author

Where to Find Help

This book is a complement to professional care, never a replacement for it. Reaching for help is a sign of strength, not weakness. If you are struggling, the resources below are free, confidential, and open to anyone. They are based in the United States; if you are somewhere else, similar services exist in most countries.

If you are in immediate danger

If you or someone else is in immediate danger, call 911, or your local emergency number, right away.

Crisis support, any time

988 Suicide and Crisis Lifeline. Call or text 988, or chat online at 988lifeline.org. It is free, confidential, and available 24 hours a day, every day, for anyone in emotional distress or crisis. You do not have to be suicidal to reach out. Veterans can press 1, and Spanish speakers can press 2.

Crisis Text Line. Text HOME to 741741 to reach a trained crisis counselor any time, free and confidential.

Substance use and mental health

SAMHSA National Helpline. Call 1-800-662-HELP (4357), or TTY 1-800-487-4889. It is a free, confidential, around-the-clock treatment referral and information service, in English and Spanish, for people and families facing substance use or mental health challenges. You can also search for treatment at findtreatment.gov.

Information and ongoing support

NAMI HelpLine (National Alliance on Mental Illness). Call 1-800-950-6264 or text "NAMI" to 62640, Monday through Friday. It is a free, nationwide service offering information, resources, and peer support for people living with mental health conditions and for those who care for them. Learn more at nami.org.

You don't have to have it all figured out before you ask for help. You only have to reach out once.

Notes and Further Reading

I came to the ideas in this book by living them, and only later found that researchers had been describing the same territory for decades. What follows is not proof that IdentiNova works. It is a map of the places where what I lived on my own lines up with what trained people found from the outside. If you want to go deeper into any single phase, this is where I would send you first.

Imprint

John Bowlby, *Attachment*, the first volume of his Attachment and Loss trilogy. Daniel J. Siegel, *The Developing Mind*.

Deconstruct

Aaron T. Beck, *Cognitive Therapy and the Emotional Disorders*. Albert Ellis, *A New Guide to Rational Living*.

Expose

Brené Brown, *Daring Greatly*. Bessel van der Kolk, *The Body Keeps the Score*. Gabor Maté, *In the Realm of Hungry Ghosts*.

Nullify

Stephen W. Porges, *The Polyvagal Theory*. Judith Herman, *Trauma and Recovery*.

Transcend

Viktor E. Frankl, *Man's Search for Meaning*. Abraham H. Maslow, *Motivation and Personality*.

Install

James Clear, *Atomic Habits*. Carol S. Dweck, *Mindset: The New Psychology of Success*.

Test

Albert Bandura, *Self-Efficacy: The Exercise of Control*. Angela Duckworth, *Grit: The Power of Passion and Perseverance.*

Yield

Robert Kegan, *In Over Our Heads*. Patricia E. Deegan, *Recovery: The Lived Experience of Rehabilitation*.